Moon Magic

A Handbook of

LUNAR CYCLES, LORE,
and MYSTICAL ENERGIES

BY
AURORA KANE

WELLFLEET
PRESS

To John, who has filled my life with light and magic.

Inspiring | Educating | Creating | Entertaining

Brimming with creative inspiration, how-to projects, and useful information to enrich your everyday life, Quarto Knows is a favorite destination for those pursuing their interests and passions. Visit our site and dig deeper with our books into your area of interest: Quarto Creates, Quarto Cooks, Quarto Homes, Quarto Lives, Quarto Drives, Quarto Explores, Quarto Gifts, or Quarto Kids.

© 2020 by Quarto Publishing Group USA Inc.

First published in 2020 by Wellfleet, an imprint of The Quarto Group,
142 West 36th Street, 4th Floor, New York, NY 10018, USA
T (212) 779-4972 F (212) 779-6058 www.QuartoKnows.com

Wellfleet titles are also available at discount for retail, wholesale, promotional, and bulk purchase. For details, contact the Special Sales Manager by email at specialsales@quarto.com or by mail at The Quarto Group, Attn: Special Sales Manager, 100 Cummings Center Suite 265D, Beverly, MA 01915 USA.

12

ISBN: 978-1-57715-187-6

Library of Congress Cataloging-in-Publication Data
Names: Kane, Aurora, author.
Title: Moon magic : a handbook of lunar cycles, lore, and mystical energies / by Aurora Kane.
Description: New York : Wellfleet Press, 2020. | Series: Magic series | Includes bibliographical references.
Identifiers: LCCN 2019027372 (print) | LCCN 2019027373 (ebook) | ISBN
   9781577151876 (hardcover) | ISBN 9780760365847 (ebook)
Subjects: LCSH: Magic–Handbooks, manuals, etc. | Human beings–Effect of the moon on–Handbooks,
   manuals, etc. | Moon–Religious aspects–Handbooks, manuals, etc. | Moon–Mythology–Handbooks,
   manuals, etc.
Classification: LCC BF1623.M66 K36 2020 (print) | LCC BF1623.M66 (ebook) | DDC 133.4/3–dc23
LC record available at https://lccn.loc.gov/2019027372
LC ebook record available at https://lccn.loc.gov/2019027373

Publisher: Rage Kindelsperger
Managing Editor: Cara Donaldson
Creative Director: Laura Drew
Project Editor: Keyla Pizarro-Hernández

Art Director: Cindy Samargia Laun
Cover Design: Laura Klynstra
Interior Design: Amelia LeBarron

Printed in China

Tarot cards on pages 106, 108–113: bigjom jom / Shutterstock.com

CONTENTS

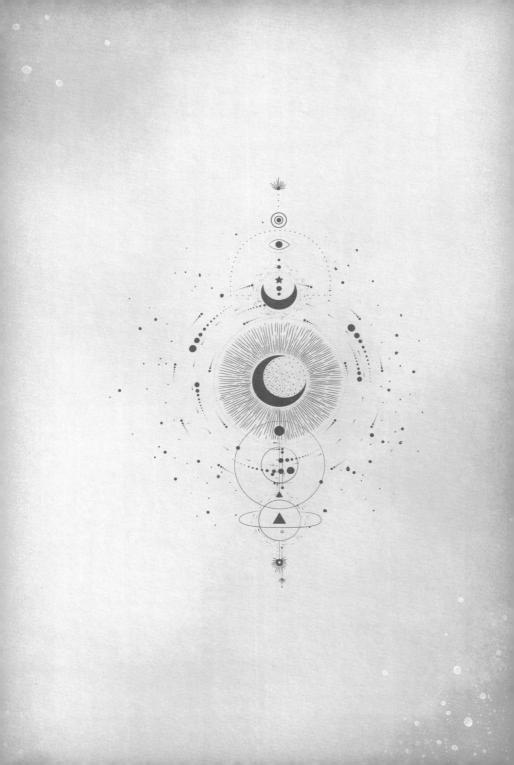

Invited all—you're welcome here, to sit and cast a spell.
But, wait—no fear, no evil here,
just lust for life lived well.

Moon's magic waits, she bides her time,
come-hither call her charms.
Her siren song, sweet lullaby, a jaunty lilting tune.

Of fortunes told or acts of bold and never-ending love.
Her light shines bright to clear our sight
and guide from up above.

Pray open mind and joyful heart, with trust unbounded be.
So drawn her way, "Don't go,"
she'll say, "we're much alike, you'll see."

Blessed be all who open these pages.
May you discover a bit of magic here to soothe or delight.

INTRODUCTION

W e all need a little magic in our lives. I'm here to help you see how the Moon—that everyday wonder-filled object that lights our skies—can help us have just that. By magic, I mean a bit of mystery, fun, enchantment, and wonder that can help us live a purposeful life connected with the natural world around us. (Nothing dark here, except the absence of light in certain lunar phases!)

You'll find the information you need to connect with the Moon and her guiding power as well as tools, tips, rituals, and spells to enhance and direct your most positive life. From health and wealth to sports and pets, from luck and love to home and career, you need look no farther than your power within to manifest your most treasured dreams.

Our gossamer Moon is not only hypnotizing, but it also makes Earth a livable place, helping stabilize climate and create tidal rhythms that have guided humans for millennia. Its most likely origin? The result of a Mars-size body colliding with Earth, whose resulting debris formed the most mesmerizing feature in our night sky—the only celestial body beyond Earth yet visited by humans.

Luna, "moon" in Latin, was the Roman Moon goddess (Selene, in Greek mythology). That goddess, the Moon, is an evocative one . . . full of luck, charm, energy, power, light—and yes, magic—inspiring love, poetry, music, literature, art, science, and more.

And this enchanting goddess has been charming us for millennia. An object of wonder, curiosity, exploration, and enlightenment, the Moon has been worshipped by people from all countries and cultures, who have looked to her for guidance, power, romance, and light.

If you're like me, at some point you've shot for the Moon, been over the Moon, howled (maybe only me?) at the Moon, been Moonstruck, hoped for the once-in-a-Blue-Moon opportunity, watched as the Man in the Moon followed you home (and wondered how he got there), even— I hope—hung the Moon for someone you love. What other inanimate object evokes such a range of emotions?

And about every twenty-nine days the Full Moon appears, as the Moon moves to the side of the Earth directly opposite the Sun, illuminated to her fullest, providing an awe-inspiring spectacle.

But what happens between these Full Moons is just as magical and powerful. Learning to understand the Moon's phases and their connection to your natural rhythms is not mysterious, but, rather, predictable, as it happens every month. How the mystical Moon influences you and the world around you as well as how you choose to harness her power to enhance your life are much more variable—and rewarding.

We know the Moon affects tides—they rise and fall with her phases. Because the human body is about 60 percent water, the Moon's pull can affect us in those same ways . . . changing the tides of our moods and intents. Harness that unique power to bring clarity to your life and positive energy to all you do. Give thanks for the Moon's guidance and influence each day by recognizing her presence in your life.

Harmonizing your natural rhythms with the Moon's is a chance to add some quiet time to your life—to break away from the constant bombardment of noise and information everywhere you look, and look, instead, into the hypnotic light of the Moon and deep into your heart and mind to determine or remind yourself what matters, to reset your compass and evaluate your path forward. It is in the quiet that we hear our thoughts most clearly.

When you align your life with the cycles of Nature and the intuitive messages of the moment, you'll find peace, deeper meaning, and increased opportunity! Remember, the Moon is full of magical power, but the power to harness it and use it wisely is within you.

THE
MAGICAL
MOON

— AND —

HER
POWERS

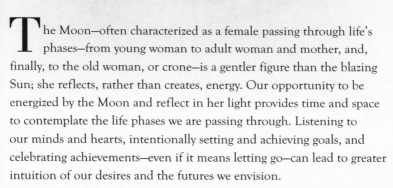

The Moon—often characterized as a female passing through life's phases—from young woman to adult woman and mother, and, finally, to the old woman, or crone—is a gentler figure than the blazing Sun; she reflects, rather than creates, energy. Our opportunity to be energized by the Moon and reflect in her light provides time and space to contemplate the life phases we are passing through. Listening to our minds and hearts, intentionally setting and achieving goals, and celebrating achievements—even if it means letting go—can lead to greater intuition of our desires and the futures we envision.

The idea of the Moon as magical stems from this idea that the Moon's phases, her monthly cycle, as well as the waxing and waning of life itself, are all interconnected. Practicing Moon magic means attuning with Nature and your natural rhythms and aligning to the energies of the Moon's powerful eight phases to focus and refine what you intentionally want to invite into, or rid from, your life. It's your time each month to focus on you, to be peaceful, quiet, and thoughtful, to be fully engaged in the moment, and to think about what's important. And while some results can be immediate . . . when the stars line up, so to speak . . . manifesting the Moon's magic in your life is a process, which means time and patience.

THE FORCE
OF THE
MOON'S PHASES

Lunar forces are invisible and individual, so they're tough to prove, but a few studies have shown how the Moon affects water. Consider that adult bodies, on average, are 60 percent water (men have a slightly higher percentage than women; lean tissue contains more water than fattier tissue). Earth's water makeup is similar—about 70 percent. If you live near a body of water, you know the tides are exaggerated during a Full or New Moon. When it comes to showing the concrete and significant effects that the Moon has on humans, one small study by Swiss researchers found people have a harder time sleeping during a Full Moon, suggesting, once again, that we are affected by lunar energy.

Also, female menstrual cycles are often referred to as "moon cycles," for good reason. Research has shown more women menstruate during a New Moon than any other phase, with a menstrual cycle and a lunar cycle roughly the same length.

If you're so inclined, consider the anecdotal evidence that suggests stranger-than-usual behavior exhibited by humans during this time—increased hospital admission rates, higher incidences of crime, and just the generally observed spooky or odd behavior of some of our fellow planet inhabitants.

While science can dispute this, it cannot dispute the wonder felt when gazing at that big, bright force in the sky, or the passion of a lover's kiss under that Moon's luminous gaze, or the power you feel when you take time to thank Nature for its wonder and meditate on using that energy to take action in line with your goals.

It takes about twenty-nine days for the Moon to pass through all eight phases. The cycle begins with the New Moon, which appears dark to us, as the Moon and Sun are aligned on the same side of Earth. As the Moon orbits Earth, the Sun's light begins to reflect off it at different angles, creating the waxing and waning effects. Beginning with the New Moon, the Sun's light visibly grows, or waxes (the young woman), until the Full Moon occurs (the adult woman), the time when the side of the Moon facing Earth is fully lit by the Sun. Transitioning to the next phase (the old woman), the light decreases, or wanes, as the Moon, again, moves into shadow, ending its cycle.

Learning each phase of the Moon, understanding its relation to Nature and our rhythms, and harnessing its power to set and act on intentions are all really easier than they sound.

THE MOON'S POWERFUL EIGHT PHASES

First, let's consider the phases in relation to the particular power or meaning they can lend to your life and then match each with appropriate actions and affirmations to bring your intentions and desires to fruition. Note, to those in the Southern Hemisphere, these phases appear reversed.

PHASE 1
NEW MOON
Beginning of the cycle—cleansing

PHASE 2
WAXING CRESCENT
Growing light illuminates intentions and intuition

FIRST QUARTER MOON

Strong light brings focus to maximize intentions

PHASE 4

WAXING GIBBOUS

*Increasing excitement and energy nurture hopes and dreams
until visible in the Full Moon*

FULL MOON

Energy, abundance, fruition, gratitude;
also a time of cleansing and letting go

PHASE 6
WANING GIBBOUS

Reflection, learning, refining based on lessons learned

LAST (THIRD) QUARTER MOON

Acknowledge and release, a time of forgiveness

WANING CRESCENT, OR BALSAMIC

End of the cycle—renewal and inward reflection, in thoughtful darkness, as a new cycle begins

INTENTION SETTING

By definition, an intention is a determination to act in a certain way. The *Upanishads*, ancient Sanskrit texts contained in the *Vedas*, tell us, "You are what your deepest desire is. As your desire is, so is your intention. As your intention is, so is your will. As your will is, so is your deed. As your deed is, so is your destiny."

Intentions begin as thoughts and become actions needed to turn our dreams and desires into reality. It's the planting and tending of a seed until it blooms into that beautiful flower you cherish.

Intention setting is inner, not outer, focused: it begins with "I am" or "I will" or "I intend" . . . *you are only able to manifest your own intentions.*

This is not a constant "wish list"—rather, living intentionally is to live with purpose, one that leads to a happy, fulfilling life. Whether that's achieving monetary success, living a life of compassion, or intentionally finding joy in everyday things, it begins with knowing your desires and intentionally taking action to achieve them.

As the Moon's glow carries energy we can use with intention setting, your thoughts create their own energy. Releasing them into the Universe invites the Universe in. The beautiful thing about setting intentions is that it opens your eyes and heart to new information . . . it increases your intuition and the ability to see related opportunities you may miss in the bustle of the day.

Journaling and meditation (see pages 19 and 56 for more) can be significant ways to reach your inner thoughts and feelings and identify where your intentions lie, as intentions must be something specific you believe in and desire. Here are some examples:

I will find the job that meets my dreams.
I am going to act with courage.
I intend to seek happiness in all that I do.

Once you've set your intentions, think quietly for a moment about them. Journal your thoughts, if you like. Be grateful for the opportunities ahead.

Intentions are set powerfully during the New Moon, the most fertile time for planting new ideas and desires. Now, combine intention setting and action with the remaining powerful phases of the Moon as you move through the cycle toward your goal.

JOURNALING INTENTIONS

Whether in your dedicated journal, a notebook, or a calendar, keep track of your intentions. These, and likely the actions you take to manifest them, will change with the Moon's phases. Being able to remind yourself of your intentions and track your progress can help you coordinate with the most influential Moon phase. Don't be afraid to ask questions; write down your honest feelings and self-empowering thoughts; and notice the sense of peace and fulfillment you get when you align desires, thoughts, and actions—*intentionally.*

POSITIVE MOON AFFIRMATIONS

Affirmations are like personal mantras we can use to program and reprogram our subconscious to view or frame things in a more positive light. We all have that self-talk running through our heads throughout the day, usually telling us something negative, or criticizing us at every turn. When we consciously choose to change the conversation (and belief and behavior) to something more positive, we can do it through affirmation.

Like developing any new habit, affirmations are most helpful in changing our beliefs and behavior when used daily. Repeat them to yourself as many times as you like. Write them on sticky notes and place them around the house as reminders, or use an app on your smartphone to help.

Much like intention setting, affirmations are "I" statements—positive, meaningful to you, and present focused. For example, if you feel unlucky in love and tell yourself it's because you're not worthy, instead of the negative reaction, take time to write down your positive traits and how they contribute to any healthy relationship. Then write an affirmation to remind yourself of your goodness. Here are some examples:

> *I am smart, funny, and loved by my friends.*
> *I am curious, kind, and intuitively know how to help the people in my life.*
> *I am me and I am enough.*

Affirmations are not chores or to-do lists. So, if a bad habit is creating your self-criticism, make sure your affirmation speaks to the positive emotions that changing it will bring.

Need to be more active? An affirmation is NOT, *I will start exercising*, but, instead: *I feel confident, more positive, and have more energy when active.*

Affirmations are positive messages said consciously that can embed in our subconscious—our inner voice—and that can help you feel more confident and successful in any area of life. So, as with intention setting, dig deep to recognize where you may need help and consciously choose to change for the better. Feeling good sends out positive vibes, which attract positive vibes in return.

Now that you have your intentions and affirmations set, you can use the Moon's phases to guide your actions and thoughts. Combining intention, actions, and affirmations is a powerful potion to add to the Moon's energy. With a little work and some focused thought, there's no limit to what you can achieve.

NEW MOON
This is the time to set intentions.

Action: Initiate a new relationship, look for a new job, get that new haircut to create a new you! Say hello, send a smile, write a note, have a conversation, kiss. Pay attention to new people who enter your life.

Affirmation: *Light a pink candle and say:* I welcome new opportunities and experiences.

WAXING CRESCENT
Reflect on your set intentions and the actions needed to manifest them.

Action: This time of gathering energy is a great time to expand on things in your life. Schedule that interview, or take a class to learn something new. Ask for what you need.

Affirmation: I have worked hard for this raise and deserve it.

FIRST QUARTER MOON
Take further appropriate actions as energies build.

Action: Nurture relationships—whether family, friends, colleagues, or lovers. Take a look around and tend to that love, which also may require pruning a few branches.

Affirmation: I am worthy of my love first, which can then be shared.

WAXING GIBBOUS
Turn up the heat—this is the home stretch.

Action: Make an offer, accept a proposal, put in the extra effort needed to complete a task. This is the time for the hard work that keeps relationships thriving, and to fuel your passion— whatever it may be.

Affirmation: My presence brings meaning to the world.

FULL MOON
Evaluate your results and celebrate your achievements.

Action: Accept congratulations, show gratitude for your accomplishments, take time to enjoy the moment, let go of thoughts and ideas not aligned with your goals. Take a breath; celebrate. Consider what may still need work.

Affirmation: I am successful even when I fail.

WANING GIBBOUS
Assess what went well and what went wrong, and share your story.

Action: Ask for help, be receptive to feedback and change, embrace the opportunities that lie ahead. This is also the time to dissolve unproductive relationships or recharge existing ones.

Affirmation: I am happy yet open to change.

LAST (THIRD) QUARTER

Freely let go of anything that is not a positive force in your life or that obstructs your goals.

Action: Stop negative thoughts, let go of hurtful habits, remove obstacles or negative people from your path. In this time of rest and reflection, take some "me" time, which all relationships need.

Affirmation: I am enough.

WANING CRESCENT

Refocus your goals and get ready to reset intentions.

Action: Embrace the darkness and the quiet, and renew and prepare for a new cycle to begin. As a new phase of intention setting begins, do not fear the unknown.

Affirmations: I am strong. I am powerful. I am here and I will thrive.

THE
FULL MOON
— AND OTHER —
MAGICAL
MOON
PHASES

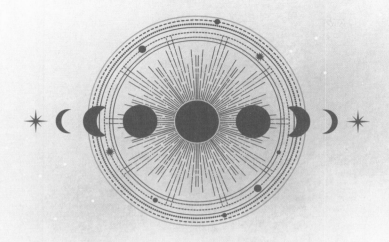

I t's hard to imagine now, but the Moon, especially the Full Moon, was a significant source of light at night, guiding travelers across uncharted seas or just across the meadows, and allowing work to continue later in the day as harvest grew near—and likely appeared as a magical lantern to ancient cultures.

Inspiring tales of ghosts, goblins, werewolves, and lunatics, the Moon also had significant effects, though not scientifically known then, on tides, weather, harvests, and Nature. It's no wonder the Full Moon is deemed meaningful around the world and throughout history. And not only that, but imagine the fear you might have felt during a lunar eclipse, when that steady Moon suddenly faded from the sky?

Here we'll look at not only the Full Moon but also some related phases, such as the Blue Moon and Black Moon, as well as lunar eclipses, which occur during the Moon's full phase.

Native Americans, who used the Moon as a calendar of sorts to track the seasons, assigned symbolic names to each month's Full Moon based on observations they made between Nature and its correlation with the Moon above. I've given each a spell to prompt your thinking to align the Full Moon's significance to your daily life.

JANUARY

Full Moon's Historical Name: Wolf Moon

Less Common Name: Old Moon

Historical Significance: January's cold and dark leave Nature's food sources in scarce supply. Howling, hungry wolves are said to be the inspiration for the name of January's Moon.

Today's Magical Significance: Consider honoring January's Moon with purposeful gratitude for bountiful food and clean water supplies, and aim to serve those less fortunate.

Moon, shine bright that I may always find food to feed my body, mind, and soul. I give thanks for your nourishing energy.

FEBRUARY

Full Moon's Historical Name: Snow Moon

Less Common Name: Hunger Moon

Historical Significance: A typically snowy month in many parts of North America gave this Moon her fitting name.

Today's Magical Significance: With colder temperatures in many areas, and increased time inside, consider basking in the Full Moon's glow while observing Nature's beautiful winter landscape. Honor your individual beauty and gifts at this time, too.

Brilliant Moon, relieve winter's darkness that descends over sky and spirit. Let beauty abound in all that I do.

MARCH

Full Moon's Historical Name: Worm Moon
Less Common Name: Sap Moon
Historical Significance: As the sap flows and the earth softens with warming temperatures, earthworms are busy at work.
Today's Magical Significance: Absorb the energy of March's Full Moon as all in Nature begins to emerge from hibernation. Consider what you have been putting off and commit to achieving your goals.

Fair Moon, awaken my heart, lest time be gone too fast.
Fair Moon, awaken my eyes to conquer my goals at last.

◀ OCCURRING AFTER THE SPRING EQUINOX ▶

APRIL

Full Moon's Historical Name: Pink Moon
Less Common Name: Sprouting Grass / Egg / Fish Moon
Historical Significance: April's Moon heralds the first spring blossoms, whose name honors early blooming wildflowers.
Today's Magical Significance: Let April's Full Moon inspire beauty in all you see and do. Acknowledge the Moon's influence with a smile to a neighbor or kind word to a friend. Save a kind word for yourself as well.

Let no fool, this April I be, without a kind word for all I see.
Your blossoming light reveals beauty no end. With song in my heart,
I feel thankful, dear friend.

MAY
Full Moon's Historical Name: Flower Moon
Less Common Name: Corn Planting / Milk Moon

Historical Significance: A time of abundance in Nature, when life is in full bloom.

Today's Magical Significance: Offer thanks to the Universe for all that is good and full in your life. May's Full Moon is a good time to be present, in the moment, to accept her rewards.

O' Moon, among stars, your beams I behold—
your shimmering arms do gently enfold.
Gather me up that grace I may feel,
for all in my life shines brightly like gold.

JUNE
Full Moon's Historical Name: Strawberry Moon
Less Common Name: Rose Moon

Historical Significance: In North America, the strawberry harvest typically occurs. In earlier days, it was the time to harvest wild strawberries.

Today's Magical Significance: When June's Full Moon is above, set an intention to savor life's flavorful moments to their fullest—no matter how humble or grand.

Full Moon, fill me with strength where I fail, joy where I succeed,
and courage to continue the fight.

JULY

Full Moon's Historical Name: Buck Moon
Less Common Name: Thunder Moon

Historical Significance: Male deer, whose antlers shed earlier in the year, have now regrown them.

Today's Magical Significance: Drawing on the alternative name, Thunder Moon, pay attention to possible energy shifts—often in opposing directions. Stay focused, but be open to change and new information. Clarity may be insightful at this time.

Mystic Moon, whose guiding presence has shown throughout the ages,
by foot or by sea or imagined it be, each journey is unlike another.
Instill in me the clarity to walk my path uncluttered.

AUGUST

Full Moon's Historical Name: Sturgeon Moon
Less Common Name: Green Corn Moon

Historical Significance: The sturgeon are in full run, as observed by North American fishing tribes.

Today's Magical Significance: Let the Moon's light illuminate the bounty in your life. Take stock of what you may be missing and set intentions to reap the benefits surrounding you.

Bountiful Moon, I ask that you fill the world with kindness, peace, and prosperity,
and the generosity to recognize and help those in need.

SEPTEMBER
Full Moon's Historical Name: Harvest Moon
Less Common Name: Barley Moon

Historical Significance: The time for harvest—the Moon's bright light also helped farmers work late into the night.

Today's Magical Significance: Consider what you may need more time to accomplish. Absorb the Moon's energy to light your way. This may be a marvelous night for that Moon dance (see page 126).

Your song of night sings quietly, sweet melody I hear. Enticed—
I sway, I dance, I pray. Dear Moon, help guide my way.

◄── OCCURRING AFTER THE AUTUMNAL EQUINOX ──►

OCTOBER
Full Moon's Historical Name: Hunter's Moon
Less Common Name: Travel Moon

Historical Significance: Fattened game, visible in the harvested fields and barren woods, offered hunters the chance to harvest food for the winter; bright light means longer hunting times.

Today's Magical Significance: October's Full Moon can illuminate where you need to "stock up" for the winter. Whatever the issue, dig deep into your inner reserves and feed your soul with kindness and encouragement. Take a moment to honor those who have nourished you along the journey.

A Hunter's Moon reminds us how our work is never done.
Waste not a day, though, stop and say, I've not done this alone.

NOVEMBER
Full Moon's Historical Name: Beaver Moon
Less Common Name: Frost Moon

Historical Significance: A time to set beaver traps before water freezes; beavers are also busy building dams.

Today's Magical Significance: Like the beavers in their dam, now may be a good time for a Moon bath (see page 126). Relax, give yourself over to the power of the Moon, and feel her balancing energy.

A break I seek to calm the mind and quiet restless days.
Send moonbow beams to whisper dreams and carry me away.

DECEMBER
Full Moon's Historical Name: Cold Moon
Less Common Name: Long Night Moon / Moon Before Yule

Historical Significance: In most parts of the Northern Hemisphere, December ushers in winter and its icy charms. Growth slows and activity wanes.

Today's Magical Significance: Take time to let the Full Moon's light warm your soul until the weather's warm breezes can warm your face.

Though ice may hang from eaves above,
your warmth shines bright and true.
Keep watch above as night grows long,
that love doth see us through.

THE BLUE MOON

Once in a Blue Moon . . . yes, that rare occurrence we hope and wish for is real—and really not quite that rare. Each calendar year, the Moon completes her final cycle about eleven days before Earth finishes its complete orbit around the Sun. These days add up, and, every two and a half years or so, there is an extra Full Moon in a given month. That second Full Moon is the *Blue Moon*.

So, yes, a Blue Moon exists, but is it blue? Well, no, the Moon is not blue (nor made of cheese!), but it can appear that way. In 1883, when the Indonesian volcano Krakatoa erupted, the blast sent ash plumes high into the atmosphere containing ash particles just the right (small) size to disperse the Sun's red light waves. So when the Moon's white beams shone through the clouds, they appeared blue. Smaller-scale volcanic eruptions, and even large wildfires, can produce similar effects.

What does the Blue Moon signify? Greater power, like the already powerful Full Moon multiplied to boost your work, supercharge your batteries, and intensify your efforts to reach your goals. It may also represent a time of intense satisfaction, as goals are met and intuition is at its height.

While the name's origin is unclear, it's certainly worth a toast with an aptly named beer for good luck, or take advantage of an extra cycle of intention setting to further your goals.

THE BLACK MOON

The Black Moon is the Blue Moon's twin sister, in a way. We experience the Full Moon when the side of the Moon facing Earth is fully lit by the Sun, and that second Full Moon in any month is known as a Blue Moon.

As the Moon dances through her phases—waxing to full and waning to new—it becomes darker. The New Moon is the time when the Earth-facing side is dark, fully in shadow. It is traditionally a time of cleansing, letting go, and setting new intentions. The *Black Moon* is that second New Moon occurring in any given month.

The Black Moon is your lunar chance to see your inner self clearly, to listen to the voice you try to ignore during times when you are too busy to pay attention. It is a time to recognize what you want and need and seek out new beginnings.

The Black Moon is said to be a time of powerful inner truth. Look deep into your soul. Do not disregard the voice inside. The Black Moon will guide you.

LUNAR ECLIPSES

Though many cultures throughout history worshipped the Sun, believing it to be most powerful, the Moon inspired her own veneration—and even fear. Eclipses were viewed by many as times of fear and bad luck. Tales abound about lunar eclipses, including such things as the Moon being eaten by a jaguar, or attacked by angry dogs and snakes . . . and even that an eclipse was an attack on ancient kings. Ancient rituals were designed to appease, or drive away, the Moon and ward off any lurking evil.

Lunar eclipses happen during a Full Moon, and most calendar years see two or three within them. These are Nature's way of getting our attention and reminding us how spectacular it is. They also shake us out of "the routine" and spark transformation. These are times of demarcation, usually signifying an ending and significant, often unexpected, change. Emotions can run high and a lunar eclipse may not be the best time for decisive action, which may not lead to the desired results. Let the energy settle for a day or two before making any important decisions and acting on them.

Tune in to your intuition. Listen to messages received from all parts of your life and take them seriously. Do not ignore them. Whether immediately or down the road, these will influence you.

CULTURAL BELIEFS, GODDESSES, AND WICCA

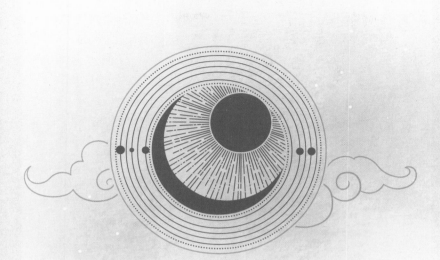

Throughout the centuries, the Moon has been regarded both as a deity and as a planet. Cultural beliefs and historical significance vary—from the mystical to the romantic. However, the Moon, in all phases, never ceases to cause a slight catch of your breath and inspire sheer wonder at her beauty, as well as respect at humans' ability to explore it. Imagine its significance centuries ago, when its presence, change, and disappearance from the sky—explainable now—was unexplainable, or darkness overtook the day with no relief to banish the fear—except from the sky . . . the Moon.

When many look at the Moon they see a gentle old soul, the Man in the Moon, staring back at them. Some cultures see a rabbit—one charged with very important goddess maintenance. There have also been reported sightings of dogs, toads, and an old woman . . . whatever you see is sure to bring delight. Here we look at the two most frequent images seen when gazing on the Moon's lovely countenance.

MAN IN THE MOON

In the Northern Hemisphere, we all know the Man in the Moon, that smiling beacon in the sky, who has inspired numerous myths and stories.

A long-told European tale says the man committed a crime: caught gathering sticks on the Sabbath—a designated day of rest—and, so, was banished to the Moon for such insurgency. Mr. Man in the Moon has been there for centuries toting those sticks and inspiring legend.

Some Germanic cultures believe the man was caught stealing from a neighbor—again, on a Sunday, the day of rest, doubling his crime—which earned him the same banishment! Germans living along the coast closely observed the Moon's influence on the tides, believing the Man in the Moon was a giant, pouring water on Earth to create the tides.

Turning to Norse legend, we learn the man kidnapped two children and carried them to heaven, only to have them fetch water with a bucket, bearing an uncanny resemblance to the story we know as "Jack and Jill."

There is a Roman legend contending he stole sheep.

The Dutch call him an unhappy vegetable thief!

Alaskan Inuits believe the Man in the Moon is the keeper of souls and that shamans can ascend to meet them.

Malaysian legend holds the Man in the Moon likes to fish, and braids bark into fishing line to catch everything on Earth—but, a rat gnaws the line and a cat chases the rat, restoring the eternal balance, so Earth is spared.

Science tells us the Man in the Moon is the aftermath of billions-of-years-old powerful asteroid collisions, whose shockwaves triggered lunar volcanic eruptions. The craters resulting from the asteroids' impact filled with volcanic magma, which, when cooled, left dark areas on the Moon's surface. These dark areas, known as lunar *maria*, or lunar seas, when the Moon is illuminated at its fullest, contrast with lighter areas on her surface and reveal that kindly face we know so well.

MOON RABBIT

Rather than the man living on the Moon, Chinese folklore holds that a rabbit lives there, where, with his mortar and pestle, he eternally grinds the magical elixir of life for the deities—particularly the Moon goddess, Chang'e. In Japan and Korea, it is believed the rabbit grinds ingredients for rice cakes.

A Native American Cree legend offers the tale of a young rabbit wishing a ride to the Moon. Borne there by the crane—the lone volunteer—the rabbit held tightly to the crane's legs, stretching and lengthening them, as the long journey unfolded. On reaching the Moon, the grateful rabbit touched the crane's head with a bleeding paw, leaving the crane's distinctive red crown. Those who believe say, on clear nights, you can see the rabbit riding the Moon.

MYTHOLOGY AND THE MOON GODDESS

In many cultures, the Moon is represented as a goddess, celebrated as a powerful female figure variously responsible for fertility, childbirth, mothering, and healing and also possessing qualities of compassion and great wisdom. For centuries, people have used the Moon's phases to determine planting and harvesting times, or looked to her as a guide for personal fertility issues.

And, as noted earlier, female menstrual cycles are often referred to as "moon cycles." You don't have to be female or menstruating, however—all of us, no matter what our identity or life stage, can utilize the Moon's magical power to release our inner goddess. As entire books have been written on this subject, the following is but a sampling to reveal a sliver of the Moon's effect on people throughout time.

GREEK MOON GODDESSES

Greek mythology comprises stories of gods and goddesses, heroes and war, rituals and natural phenomena, whose influence was widely felt in everyday life—and made lasting impact on the arts, literature, architecture, and music of the culture.

Selene: This Titan goddess, revered as the personification of the Moon, is often depicted wearing a crescent Moon on her head, riding her chariot across the sky, pulling the Moon. She was worshipped at the New and Full Moons, believed to have the power to light the sky and render sleep.

Artemis: Closely associated with the Full Moon (her brother, Helios, was the Sun god), she is also connected with the hunt, Nature, and childbirth.

Hecate: A dog-loving crone, goddess of the waning and dark Moons, is often depicted carrying a torch—symbolic of her great wisdom. Among her numerous associations are entrances; placing a shrine at an entrance—whether to a structure or city—was believed to hinder evil spirits from entering.

ROMAN MOON GODDESSES

Roman mythology, being heavily influenced by Greek mythology, also contains numerous gods and goddesses. These myths were ways of interpreting mortals' relationships with the natural world and explaining the unexplainable, tackling tough issues such as the afterlife and good versus evil.

Luna: Luna is the Roman equivalent of the Greek's Selene, the goddess of the Moon personified, and also worshipped at the New and Full Moons.

Diana: The Romans worshipped Diana as goddess of the hunt and wild animals. As Sun god Apollo's (the Roman version of Helios) twin sister, she came to be associated with the Moon—responsible for fertility and childbirth.

NATIVE AMERICAN MOON GODDESSES

As we've explored (see pages 28 to 33), Native Americans assign a special significance to the Moon. Their deep respect and connection with Nature aligned with the Moon's phases as it guided their day-to-day existence. It is a symbol of protection and serenity, one honored also in association with Moon goddesses.

Komorkis: Honored by the Blackfoot tribe, Komorkis is the wife of the Sun god Natosi, and mother of the stars.

Hanwi: This Oglala Sioux goddess was believed to have lived with the Sun god, Wi. He took displeasure with her, forcing her to become a creature of the night.

CHINESE MOON GODDESSES

For centuries, the Chinese people have gathered in fall to give thanks for the harvest. Today, they celebrate during the famous Mid-Autumn, or Moon, Festival that occurs on the fifteenth day of the eighth lunar Moon—when the Moon is at her largest and brightest in the sky. The celebration is built widely around the legend of Moon goddess Chang'e. Brightly colored lanterns and delicious Moon cakes only add to the festivities.

Chang'e: After drinking the magical elixir of immortality to save it from evil hands, beautiful Chang'e ascended into the heavens and chose the Moon as her new home. If you look hard enough, it is said, you can still see her there.

Kuan Yin: The Buddhist goddess of the Moon, compassion, and healing.

AZTEC MOON GODDESS

The Aztecs were fairly sophisticated in their observations of celestial events. And, like other cultures, they used myths and stories to help explain the phenomena they witnessed.

Coyolxauhqui: A rather gruesome story of how the Moon came to be: Coatlicue (goddess of life and death) had a daughter, Coyolxauhqui—and

400 sons! Coatlicue, mysteriously, became pregnant and was thought to have disgraced her children. Coyolxauhqui convinced her brothers to kill their mother, but her unborn child, Huitzilopochtli (the Sun god), having learned of the plot, sprang from her womb as a grown adult equipped for battle and killed his sister, Coyolxauhqui. He cut her into pieces and tossed her head into the sky, where it now hangs as the Moon.

MAYAN MOON GODDESS

The Mayan people had no shortage of gods and goddesses to ask for help—more than 250 in all—and these deities were involved in all aspects of daily life, from birth to death.

Ixchel: The goddess, Ixchel, which translates to "Lady Rainbow," was, among other things, goddess of the Moon, love, and gestation and provider of rain to nourish the crops. Her beauty and femininity are said to have given her Moon goddess status. She faced many challenges in life with grace and perseverance and reminds us of our power to take charge and face what comes.

INDIAN MOON GODDESS

The ancient Indian peoples, as elsewhere throughout the world, found solace and wonder in the Moon's bright light. However, that light was not constant, like the Sun's, and came to represent rebirth and the world of their ancestors' souls.

Candi: Candi was Chandra's female counterpart, and the two alternated monthly in filling the role of the Moon.

EGYPTIAN MOON GODDESSES

The population of ancient Egyptian gods and goddesses was impressive—totaling more than 2,000 deities in the Egyptian pantheon. Egyptian culture grew around the celebration and integration of these forces in people's everyday lives, which continued on into the afterlife.

Isis: This powerful, intuitive, and widely worshipped goddess was not only a Moon deity but also a multi-tasking Sun goddess. She was revered as a mother and fertility goddess.

Sefkhet, or Seshat: This ancient Egyptian Moon goddess was also honored as the goddess of time, architecture, and the stars. Some believe she was the wife of Thoth, one of the most important gods of ancient Egypt and creator of the alphabet.

PAGAN AND CELTIC MOON GODDESSES

The Celts and Druids have a long-held connection with Nature, and a profound reverence for it—and of ancient lore and wisdom.

Arianrhod: This Moon goddess's lovely name translates to "silver wheel"—an apt description of the Moon that descends into the sea. People looked to her for fertility issues as well as rebirth, in the many forms it can take.

Cerridwen: The crone. Though a goddess of the dark and associated with the Waning Moon, Cerridwen watchfully tended the cauldron of wisdom.

Epona: This horse goddess was associated with the night and dreams. Legends still tell of the sound of her horse's hoof beats as she rides swiftly west to escape the Sun's rising rays.

Rhiannon: A Moon goddess whose name means "night queen," Rhiannon reigned supreme over issues of fertility and death.

NORSE MOON GODDESSES

Look to the goddesses of Nordic mythology to reflect the matriarchal roles of the time. That wisdom is as relevant today to your role as mother, caregiver, or nurturer.

Elle: Depicted as the crone, this old woman is no pushover—purportedly defeating Thor in a wrestling match. She was looked to for strength and confidence.

Freya: No ordinary goddess, Freya held a significant position in the goddess pecking order. She was revered for her beauty and is said to have influence in the areas of love, wealth, fertility, and magic, among others.

Frigg: Her significant duties included being goddess of marriage, childbirth, motherhood, wisdom, and weaving. Her name means "love" and she signified all things domestic tranquility.

WICCA AND
MOON MAGICK TODAY

Simply put, Wicca is a *Nature-based* pagan religion, one quite modern in its origins but that is based on ancient pre-Christian religious beliefs. The Moon represents the female goddess, both as a symbol of Earth and of fertility.

The practice of Wiccan benevolent magick (with a *k*) is about raising and directing universal energies to co-create with Nature to fulfill your intentions. Celebrations honor and unite with the natural rhythms of the seasons and Nature. Wicca is within you—you cannot find "it" outside of you—you must look within.

Wicca is so much more than "spells." It is living an intention-filled life, aligned with Nature and its energies—that is when the real magick happens, when life flows. Spells are only a tool. Their magick is in their focused energy, based on your intention setting.

The pentacle, or encircled five-pointed star, is a symbol of Wicca and witchcraft, and represents Nature's elements and spirit.

✴ At the top of the star is the Spirit, connecting you to the energy that permeates all of Nature and us—our higher consciousness.

* Moving in a clockwise direction, the next point represents Earth (directionally, north, or home). It grounds us, supports us, and shares its wisdom with us.
* Moving to the next point, clockwise, we find Air (directionally, east), representing new beginnings, ideas, and thoughts.
* Next (directionally, south) is Fire, with its passion, inner light, purpose, and desire.
* The last point on the star (directionally, west) represents Water—that vast ocean—which brings healing and speaks to our subconscious and dreams.

One of the most significant celebrations for those practicing Wicca is Esbat. It is typically held during a Full Moon (although other phases can be celebrated, if desired), to honor the Goddess Moon and work with her heightened energy, amplifying intentions set. It is a time when a coven comes together to celebrate, but it can also be celebrated in a solitary way.

Even if you're not a practicing Wiccan, follow the ceremony's format with a group of like-minded friends to honor the Goddess Moon and set intentions based on your needs.

ESBAT RITUAL

Before you begin, know there are no rules—*except, do no harm.*

Set up your altar (a space used as a visual reminder and a place to focus your energy; see page 138 for more information) outside, if possible, under the Full Moon's energizing light, with any tools (candle, crystals, natural items, photos, etc.), you want to use in your intention setting. Each participating member may contribute something. Your altar does not have to be fancy—it can be something as simple as a shoebox to hold everything (be careful here if lighting candles, choose a different location) or a small table, and it can grow as needed.

Gather your group around the altar to create a sacred space to honor the goddess. This space is usually a circle—really an orb, or sphere of energy. Cast your circle by joining hands and standing or sitting in a circle, or just draw a circle in the space with your finger to set the significance. Everyone "in" the circle is contributing to its energy. Casting simply means connecting with the energies of the Earth and Universe.

Invite the goddess into your circle. From the New to the Full Moon (waxing phases), the energies of the celebration are used to draw things *to you*. During the waning phases, post Full Moon, the energies are used to release anything that no longer serves. Working with the Full Moon, your ritual may include chants, prayers, spells, blessings, or other work based on the focus of your celebration, or a simple dance, as a circle, moving in a clockwise direction. Why clockwise? The spinning clockwise energy brings things to you. Spinning in a counterclockwise motion dispels or banishes.

⁕

The Esbat ceremony can sometimes include the drawing down of the Moon. Essentially, it is a symbolic activity that also includes the Cakes and Ale ritual.

Within the circle, the group leader fills a chalice, or other cup, with liquid—anything you like, or influenced by the season, for example, lemonade in summer, cider in fall, Champagne if celebrating a special occasion (this is the "ale" part of the ritual). She holds the cup to the Moon, reciting a prayer of choice, inviting the Goddess Moon to fill the chalice with her wisdom and energy. The chalice is then passed, in a clockwise motion, around the circle for everyone to drink from. When passed, say something like, "May you never thirst."

Continue on to share the "cakes," which can be anything from a lovely homemade seeded bread to simple store-bought cookies. As with the chalice, pass them around the group, saying something like, "May you never hunger."

The drawing down of the Moon is often concluded with the recitation of the inspirational *The Charge of the Goddess* (a popular version is by Doreen Valiente).

When finished, as a group set an intention to disband the circle, or walk counterclockwise to release its energy. Take a moment to thank the Earth for supporting you and the Moon for guiding you.

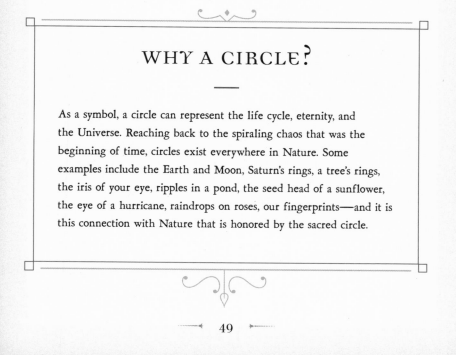

WHY A CIRCLE?

—

As a symbol, a circle can represent the life cycle, eternity, and the Universe. Reaching back to the spiraling chaos that was the beginning of time, circles exist everywhere in Nature. Some examples include the Earth and Moon, Saturn's rings, a tree's rings, the iris of your eye, ripples in a pond, the seed head of a sunflower, the eye of a hurricane, raindrops on roses, our fingerprints—and it is this connection with Nature that is honored by the sacred circle.

HARNESSING MOON MAGIC

— WITH —

HERBS AND NATURE

N ow is the time to bring the Moon's revealing, healing, energizing, and magical power into your life. Using herbs and Nature herself, we'll explore manifesting the Moon's energy to enhance your intentions and actions. The innate energies of these "natural" tools help connect to and increase your vibrational energy, and, in turn, connect you to the Moon's.

Keep in mind, with all your "magical" work, no special tools are required other than your presence and focus on setting intentions in tune with the natural rhythms surrounding you, and the Moon's phases guiding you. All else just adds to the atmosphere. So, use what you have, buy what you need, or just let your inner goddess guide your thoughts—your own intuition is the best tool in your magical bag.

COMMON HERBS
AND THEIR MEANINGS

Just as flowers have their own language . . . red rose, anyone? . . . herbs have something to say as well, and that symbolism often dates back centuries.

While almost any herb can be used as part of your Moon rituals, during any of her magical phases, it may help to choose one that supports your intentions at that particular time through its meaning. In this chapter, I list some commonly available herbs to start. Feel free to try others, always keeping in mind your intentions.

Following are some ideas for using herbs during the Moon's four main phases to capture her inherent wisdom and guidance as you seek to further your goals and manifest intentions. As you feel comfortable, expand the herbs you work with and amplify your work during the Moon's remaining monthly phases. There is no right or wrong, only what you feel, need, and want.

Note: Most herbs here are culinary herbs, but please know *not all herbs are safe for consumption,* so before venturing into teas, tinctures, or other culinary uses, discuss any internal herb use with your health care provider to be safe.

Angelica: healing, protection

Basil: wealth, courage, opening the heart for forgiveness, good intentions

Bay leaf: purification, strength, fame, reward

Camphor: divination

Chamomile: long life, money, patience, sleep

Chives: usefulness

Cinnamon: abundance, psychic powers, spirituality

Coriander: hidden assets

Dill: luck, power against evil, preservation

Fennel: courage, praiseworthy

Fenugreek: money

Garlic: exorcism, healing, protection

Heather: acceptance, rainmaking

Jasmine: abundance, prophetic dreams

Lavender: happiness, peace, virtue

Mint

Mustard

Rosemary

Lemon balm: success, sympathy

Licorice: fidelity, love, lust

Mint: refreshment, travel

Moonwort: love, money

Mugwort: prophetic dreams, psychic powers, strength

Mustard: fertility

Myrtle: fertility, fidelity, love, money

Oregano: substance

Parsley: joy, love

Rosemary: acceptance, clarity, love, remembrance

Sage: immortality, wisdom

Sandalwood: protection, spirituality

Thyme: activity, courage

Turmeric: clarity, purification

Violet: luck, peace, wishes

Willow: enchantment, love

HERBS AND THE MOON'S PHASES

NEW MOON

**Herbs to inspire and motivate at a time when energy is
starting to build and may need a boost**
Consider a blend of lemon verbena, lemon thyme, and ginger,
or try energizing peppermint alone.

WAXING MOON

**Herbs to clear the mind (and cobwebs), nourish,
and restore so you may focus on the job at hand**
Sip a cup of single-herb tea using rosemary, thyme, ginseng, or basil.

FULL MOON

**Herbs to help you let go of negative emotions
and dispel distraction to feel balanced and centered**
Blend lemongrass with ginger, or try a brew of St. John's wort.

WANING MOON

**Relaxing herbs to help you slow down, open your mind
and heart, and boost your intuition, making you receptive
to Nature's messages and signals; a time of forgiveness**
Steep lavender and chamomile and let the world's worries slip away.

MEDITATION
AND MOON MAGIC

It's widely known that spending time in and with Nature is good for the heart, mind, and soul. Feeling the warm sunlight on your face, breathing in clean, crisp air, listening to the cheerful chorus of spring birds, and smelling the blooming flowers in a garden are all simple activities that afford the chance to slow down, take a calming breath, and savor the moment. Doing so in a mindful way—meaning consciously focusing on the moment and experiencing all the thoughts and sensations that accompany or arise from it—can help calm us and enhance our overall well-being. This, in turn, can lead to increased self-confidence and fostering a purposeful life or sense of fulfillment.

All Nature's cycles generously offer their gifts. Combining these with the magical phases of the Moon helps elevate our human existence into a sacred realm. Open your arms to Mother Moon, and allow her to take you into hers.

MEDITATION BASICS

To meditate is to engage in contemplation or reflection, or to engage in a mental exercise (as in concentrating on your breathing or repeating a mantra) to reach a heightened level of spiritual awareness. Buddhists, who have been practicing meditation for millennia, believe it develops concentration, clarity, emotional positivity, and a calmness that is needed to see the truth. When you focus your thoughts, you eliminate the endless lists running through your brain that may be causing you stress or worry or that are making it hard to focus and make decisions.

There are various types of meditation. For our purposes, the form often referred to as mindful meditation, where you strive for an increased awareness of being in the moment, of experiencing thoughts, feelings, and sensations as they are now—with no preconceived notions or judgment—is what I mean.

For those today who practice meditation, it's commonly a way to relieve stress and reduce anxiety. If you've been meditating for a while, you have already experienced the positive things it can bring to your life. If not, you have nothing to lose; there is no right or wrong, and it doesn't have to take lots of time. Adding it to your Moon magic work is not required, but it offers another tool to tap into your inner thoughts and feelings that can then become intentions set to achieve your goals.

Regular meditation can bring about a transforming sense of relaxation and ease. Learning to focus your thoughts helps clear the clutter that can accumulate in our brains. It helps us see what's important and, more importantly, just *be* for a while.

Meditation has been said to contribute to overall improved physical and mental well-being, including helping develop a new perspective on stressful situations, reducing negative emotions and reactions, boosting creativity, fostering acceptance, decreasing pain, and increasing happiness. Meditation can also help develop your intuitive senses, which are helpful for all your magical work.

You don't need a lot of, or really any, fancy equipment or gear to meditate—only a quiet space (outdoors surrounded by Nature is a great option), a comfortable position, and an open mind—and maybe a gentle alarm if you prefer to time your sessions. Make this as fancy as you like, with essential oils, crystals, candles, other rituals, etc., or as simple as just breathing. Whatever you choose to make it, make it regular and stress free. No rules.

✳ In your chosen quiet, calm location, sit comfortably. Close your eyes to limit distractions.
✳ Naturally breathe in and out through your nose, focusing your attention on each in-breath and out-breath. Breathe gently and naturally—let yourself relax.

* As you concentrate on your breath, your mind may wander. Gently bring your attention back to your breath and continue to concentrate.
* Alternatively, as you continue your breathing you may scan your body, focusing your attention solely on one part before moving on to the next—starting at your toes and moving upward to your scalp. If a particular part feels tense or painful, focus your mind and breathing on that part until it is relaxed before moving on to the next. Again, if your attention wanders, gently refocus and continue the process.

MEDITATING WITH THE MOON

Meditation can be useful, and incorporated, into your Moon magic practice in numerous ways. Make it personal, make it your own, and make it fun. Here are some ideas.

* Invite your favorite Moon goddess to your next meditation session and focus on the qualities she can bring (see page 40).
* Have your favorite crystal, or other crystal whose energies you want to work with, nearby as you meditate (see page 62).
* Light a candle and diffuse some essential oils to help set the mood. Remember to set a gentle timer so the candle does not burn down all the way, and have something nearby to help extinguish it when needed.
* Use your next meditation to focus on a problem, or an opportunity, to help clear the mental pathways.
* Meditate on the intention you just set and the outcome you desire.
* Meditate under the next Full Moon to reap the greatest benefits in terms of universal energies to synchronize with.

* After journaling about an issue, meditate on what resonates most with you.
* Meditate while Moon bathing (see page 126) for the ultimate cleansing and relaxation experience.
* Meditate for five minutes every evening to thank the Moon for its magical energy and express gratitude for the day just lived.
* Meditate for insight and calm when your lunar cycle experiences bumps in the road.

HARNESSING MOON MAGIC

— WITH —

CRYSTALS AND GEMSTONES

Created through millennia in the heart of Earth, absorbing its energies and messages along with those sent by the Sun, Moon, and oceans, natural crystals and gemstones hold that power and emit those energies, helping raise your personal vibration and enhancing your psychic and intuitive powers. They contain the natural pulse of the Earth, the breath of the Earth, and they can speak to you, if you listen. Adding crystals and their unique energies to your Moon work helps you amplify her messages and harness her energies to uniquely empower your life.

When you focus your energies and intentions on your crystals, the crystals hold them there, inside, reminding you—by their very presence—what is important to you.

In addition to the inherent fire and beauty we find in crystals and gemstones, they each bring their unique power, energy—often healing—and meaning to utilize. Select the ones you work with based on your desired intentions, which means they'll change as you do, or use them just because you like them and they "resonate" with you—maybe you feel the special power of your birthstone or the unexpected connection with a particular stone given to you as a gift. Large or small, it doesn't matter. And they don't have to be expensive. Many here are commonly available.

CRYSTALS, GEMSTONES, AND MOON MAGIC

We'll look at some basic crystals to incorporate into your Moon rituals, specifically moonstone, clear quartz, selenite, moldavite, citrine, tiger's eye, green jade, rose quartz, and Himalayan salt, as well as the properties of each traditional birthstone. As your interest grows, there are numerous books on the subject to help you expand your collection.

WEARING OR CARRYING

Whether you wear your crystals—in raw form or polished or faceted—in the form of jewelry, or carry them with you is purely a matter of preference. Or just let them be, placed near you on your desk or in the room where you meditate or sleep, or on a windowsill to guard against negative energy entering your space. However you need them to be, they will be there with you. Get to know each crystal's basic personality, and select the ones you feel "in tune" with. Start basic and grow from there.

MOONSTONE
BEST MOON PHASE: ALL

Moonstone, once believed to have originated from moonbeams themselves, traditionally helps in tuning in to the natural ebb and flow of the Moon's energy and can help you embrace the wax and wane of your natural rhythms. If you're dealing with high emotions, or are in need of restoring calm and balance, this could be the stone for you. It is also one of reflection, helping you look within and find forgiveness. Moonstone comes alive under light, just as your intentions can with the Moon's light and energy. Because moonstone is a stone of new beginnings and fertility, the New Moon is a particularly fertile time to incorporate it into your Moon magic rituals. It is often associated with Zodiac water signs (see page 92).

Place your moonstone in a glass of water. Holding it up to the Moon, say quietly or aloud:

Whether yes, whether no; whether stop, whether go,
May the luminous light dance and delight,
That peace and happiness unfold.

Take time to be grateful for what you have and hopeful for what will come.

CLEAR QUARTZ
BEST MOON PHASE: FULL MOON

Clear quartz crystals are your basic, but extremely powerful, generic crystal—meaning they can take on whatever you've got to offer. Their powerful energies are particularly useful during a Full Moon, but don't let that limit your interactions with them. Be specific in your intentions when working with clear quartz and they'll absorb them fully. Be sure to listen to the energy vibes they send out in return. In a nod to its all-purpose nature, this crystal can be helpful to all signs of the Zodiac (see page 96), to amplify intentions, counteract negative energy, and find acceptance. It is also the crystal of wisdom.

When choices abound and decisions elude, seek clear quartz's power. Holding the crystal and feeling its warmth and energy, unite with the Moon's energy to amplify your focus. Say quietly or aloud:

In times like these I know I must decide what's right and true.
Pray, Moon, you might, with crystal's sight, help guide me as I choose.
In stillness here I listen now. I wait to hear my muse.

SELENITE
BEST MOON PHASE:
NEW MOON AND FULL MOON

Selenite's name honors the Greek Moon goddess, Selene. This healing and protective crystal is easy to work with and beneficial to all. It helps shift negative energies, rebalance the body, and connect with higher protective guardians. One simple use is to smudge with it—whether a space or yourself—(see page 116) to clear or release all negative energy nearby. Its cleansing energies, when paired with those of the New and Full Moons, are particularly effective to wipe the slate clean and clearly see the path forward. Selenite is also thought to promote honesty and truth, and good relationships as a result. Taurus (see page 96) is particularly attuned with selenite.

Incorporate selenite into any ritual you perform to clear the way for positive energies to take over.

When doubt and fear do lurk too near, sweep shadows out the door.
No harm shall come to anyone within your healing aura.
With Moon above and crystal charm, I feel strong and in power.

MOLDAVITE
BEST MOON PHASE: FULL MOON

A true star is born! Moldavite is among the rarest of materials on Earth.
Used as a gem, but more of a glass, technically, this highly vibrational
crystal was born from a huge meteorite collision with the Earth about
fifteen million years ago. The Czech Republic, near the Moldau River
(hence the stone's name), is the single source of this transformative stone.
Its energies are said to bring healing, particularly connecting the mind
and heart, unearth or increase intuitive abilities, effect swift change,
and boost energy. As it is born of the stars, every sign of the Zodiac may
benefit from its use.

> The immense intensity of moldavite makes it particularly
> good for meditation as part of your Moon rituals. Its extreme
> vibrational energy can bring even more profound results and
> help usher in the change you seek.

> *Stone born of the heavens, guide my earthly stay.*
> *Moonbeams borne through darkness, gently light the way.*
> *Bring the change I seek, or change my thoughts, I pray*
> *That heart and mind intuit, life's part that I'm to play.*

CITRINE
BEST MOON PHASE: NEW MOON, WAXING MOON, AND FULL MOON

This lovely sunny-colored stone instills optimism and attracts prosperity. Newfound or enhanced wealth can certainly be in the form of spendable cash, but also realized from a happy, healthy life. The New Moon and Full Moon phases, of new beginnings and abundance, respectively, are perfect times to include citrine in your rituals.

Spend a minute focusing your intentions on the citrine. Keep it with you the entire lunar cycle, whether in your wallet, on your desk, or wearing it. When ready, say quietly or aloud:

For health:

> *Generous, abundant, joyful Moon, enrich my life today.*
> *A happy me, will gladly be much richer without strife.*

For wealth, or at least a boost in income:

> *Full Moon, wealth indeed is what I seek, for family, friends, and me.*
> *Cast your light on my request, that rich, yes, I may be.*

Take a moment to be quietly grateful for the riches currently abundant in your life.

TIGER'S EYE
BEST MOON PHASE: WAXING GIBBOUS

Tiger's eye, aptly named, is reputed to give the ability to see, observe, and sense, and to bring differing views into a harmonious picture—another set of eyes on the problem. It releases fear and anxiety, instills confidence to act, and provides the will to follow through. Tiger's eye energies align naturally with the Moon's Waxing Gibbous phase, when energy and excitement build, and a little clarity can offer another perspective. Capricorns, with their intense productivity inclination, may find this stone useful.

Hold a tiger's eye and say quietly or aloud:

Bright and shining tiger's eye, lend me your power
To see around corners and know it's the hour
When planning and action do meet and require
Great courage and wisdom to fulfill desire.

GREEN JADE
BEST MOON PHASE: ALL

Green jade brings wealth and prosperity and extreme good luck, and is thought to protect the loving heart. Call on green jade at any time during the Moon's cycle, but expect the Full Moon to bring realization of your intentions. Libras may find this stone particularly appealing.

Hold a green jade and say quietly or aloud:

> *They say that jade was made for luck; the Moon nods, "I agree."*
> *It's luck I need—no room for chance. So, please, do honor me*
> *That with your help good karma knocks and "in luck" I may be!*

ROSE QUARTZ
BEST MOON PHASE:
WAXING AND WANING GIBBOUS

Rose quartz is the stone of unconditional love—for yourself and others. This is another great stone for Libras, but we all need and want love, and self-love is the place to start. Good vibes attract good vibes and you could soon find your romantic dreams a reality. Rose quartz is best used during the Waning Gibbous phase, fostering feelings of love and gratitude as the Moon's cycle comes to a close.

Carry a rose quartz with you and use it to channel the Moon's loving energy any time you need it. For an extra boost, say quietly or aloud:

Loving warmth from up above, look kindly on my heart.
Send through space your fond embrace and words to reassure.
Point me on the path to find love's greatest gift of all.

HIMALAYAN SALT
BEST MOON PHASE: NEW MOON

Yes, Himalayan salt is actually a crystal—and one fully infused with ancient vibrational energies of the oceans and Earth, where it has been growing for more than 250 million years—and a powerful tool to raise your personal vibrations. It contains more than eighty trace elements and minerals that our bodies need. Its vibrational properties are similar to rose quartz, and it offers cleansing and protection from negative energies. Known for its healing properties, Himalayan salt is a true gift from Mother Nature.

Whether sprinkled on a homemade cookie, kicking up the rim of a handcrafted Margarita, or scattered in a bath (see page 126) to soothe and calm, Himalayan salt from the Earth below and the Moon's vast wisdom from the sky above, create a magical recipe. Whatever ritual you choose, look to the Moon and, when ready, say quietly or aloud:

> *Heal, protect, and energize, this salt of Earthly stores*
> *That life tastes fresh and new and best when each day is adored.*
> *I hear the music laugh and play, a message from the Moon:*
> *She says today, do not delay, dance to life and love's sweet tune.*

BIRTHSTONE ENERGIES AND MOON MAGIC

Incorporating your birthstone into crystal work along with the power of the Moon's phases increases those good vibrational energies, which you may be able to sense more strongly. Wearing your birthstone is said to bring good luck and good health. The list that follows is based on the traditional stones associated with each birth month and some suggestions for how their individual energies may support your Moon magic.

FULL MOON RECHARGE

Just as we need time to recharge, or reset ourselves, as in a good night's sleep, relaxing vacation, or simple alone time, crystals benefit from the same. No, I'm not saying take them on vacation with you; simply recharging/retuning them under that magical light of a Full Moon can do the trick, or place them in a glass of water overnight (only those that are water friendly) with a pinch of Himalayan salt to bathe in the Moon's light. There is no guideline for how often to do this; you may sense when they need a cleansing (if you work with them regularly, you'll be in tune with their energy). So, place them where they can absorb the energy from the Full Moon's light and they'll do the rest of the work and be ready to use again when you need them—fully recharged.

JANUARY
GARNET

———

Meaning: Garnet is believed to keep its wearer safe while traveling.
Energy: Powerfully energizing and revitalizing, it also purifies and invites love and devotion.

Hold a garnet and say quietly or aloud:
When wanderlust strikes and travel you must, keep garnet at hand until journey's end. From start to finish, its wearer will be delivered back home the wiser to be.

FEBRUARY
AMETHYST

———

Meaning: At one time, only available to royalty, this stone is thought to build relationships. It is also said to guard against intoxication (maybe a good choice for the Moon dance party!).
Energy: Amethyst has a strong healing/calming vibration, boosts inner strength, and offers spiritual protection.

Hold an amethyst and say quietly or aloud:
Cast out worry and doubt, no matter the source, with amethyst worn, please, close to one's heart. One glance and you'll know this color's true charms lie in taming the demons and healing the mind.

MARCH
AQUAMARINE

———

Meaning: Drinking the water in which this stone has been soaked was believed to cure heart, liver, and stomach ailments.
Energy: Aquamarine helps with anger release, stress reduction, and the courage to take what life throws at you.

Hold an aquamarine and say quietly or aloud:
When life throws a curveball, remember to breathe, and reach for this stone with its water-like sheen. Imagine you're floating above all the fray, 'til reaching still waters where safe you can stay.

APRIL
DIAMOND

———

Meaning: This symbol of everlasting love is also believed to instill courage (makes sense, those two go together). However, a diamond worn for effect or prestige will bring the opposite in love.
Energy: A natural amplifier of physical and spiritual energies, this stone never needs recharging.

Hold a diamond and say quietly or aloud:
A diamond shines bright, its brilliant display, to bring your unique beauty out into play. Send with its gleam your message of love, or seek in its sparkle the essence of truth.

MAY
EMERALD
———

Meaning: The emerald is a sign of wisdom, growth, and patience.
Energy: This stone helps release negative energy and opens your heart to love and the power of inner strength.

Hold an emerald and say quietly or aloud:
When eager we are to reach the next phase, seek emerald's charms to help guide the way.

JUNE
PEARL
———

Meaning: The pearl is a traditional symbol of purity and inner wisdom.
Energy: While not a true crystal, pearls can be worn to magnify loyalty, truth, and sincerity.

Hold a pearl and say quietly or aloud:
The shimmering glow of a pearl in your hand. The softness, the roundness—perfection—remind you of love at its height. For love of one's self and truth to your heart are seen in this gift from the sea.

JULY
RUBY
————

Meaning: Ruby's red color symbolizes love and passion.
Energy: This stone's glorious color promotes energy, sensuality, and vitality.

Hold a ruby and say quietly or aloud:
When passionate love fills the air, ruby's red color ignites. As wearer—beware—for others may stare as your energy dazzles the night.

AUGUST
PERIDOT
————

Meaning: Peridot symbolizes strength.
Energy: This stone helps usher in prosperity and peace.

Hold a peridot and say quietly or aloud:
The color of green has always brought luck, and peridot's hue is the same. The luck, in this case, is the calm on your face and the courage and strength in your heart.

SEPTEMBER
SAPPHIRE
—

Meaning: Sapphire is another symbol of purity and wisdom.

Energy: Sapphire's energy has a calming effect. Work with it to strengthen belief in yourself and foster self-esteem.

Hold a sapphire and say quietly or aloud:
Cool as a cucumber—that's what they say—but, cool as a sapphire can help ease the day.

OCTOBER
OPAL
—

Meaning: The opal represents faithfulness and confidence.

Energy: This stone encourages creativity and emits a protective aura.

Hold an opal and say quietly or aloud:
With colors aflame that shift in the light, no wonder this stone does entrance. Chameleon its charms, they shift and disarm, its wearer feels strong, free, and bright.

NOVEMBER
TOPAZ
——

Meaning: Topaz symbolizes love and affection.
Energy: This stone promotes honesty, inner wisdom, and openness.

Hold a topaz and say quietly or aloud:
This golden-hued stone, as bright as the Sun, can light up your world with its fire. Seek all that you need when wearing this charm, from wisdom to love to desire.

DECEMBER
TURQUOISE
——

Meaning: Turquoise is believed to bring luck and good fortune.
Energy: This healing stone heightens your spiritual attunement and promotes clear communication.

Hold a turquoise and say quietly or aloud:
The Full Moon and turquoise in harmony blend, to sing sweet a song of the siren. Listen, I pray, you'll hear what they say, and sway to the message in rhythm.

HARNESSING MOON MAGIC

— WITH —

ESSENTIAL OILS AND CANDLES

If you'd like to add an element of fun to your Moon magic that stimulates the senses as well, consider incorporating essential oils and candles. The oils' soothing, uplifting, or energizing scents can be used to match your mood or intentions, and the candles add vibrational color power as well as ambience to any spell or ritual you're working on.

Essential oils, also known as volatile oils, are natural oils that are, essentially, the essence of the plant from which they were extracted, such as lavender essential oil. They contain the flavor, aroma, and energies of the live plants and are versatile in their uses.

Various popular uses of essential oils include smelling or diffusing their energizing properties for their effect on everything from mood to libido to headaches, rubbing them onto your body, placing in a soothing bath, or adding to other creams and oils to use on the body.

When purchasing oils, you'll find lots of choices. Look for oils that are pure, with no additives.

Light and oxygen deteriorate oils, so store them in dark glass bottles, in a cool, dark place. If you notice any change to the oil at all, discard it.

As we learned with herbs (see page 52), using the natural properties and energies of essential oils can be coordinated with the Moon's changing energies for ritual work or spells. Achieving results starts with knowing your desires and setting intentions accordingly. Let's look at the Moon's four main phases for ideas on how to use essential oils to increase good vibrations. (See page 86 for caution instructions).

NEW MOON

Soak up the Moon's inspiring and motivating energies at a time when overall energy is just starting to build and may need a boost to get going. This is a time to instill confidence to face new initiatives. Energy-boosting and motivational essential oils include:

Cedarwood, to help improve sleep, giving you more energy the next day.

Ginger, for its circulation-improving abilities and the ability to maintain energy levels.

Sunny citrus, such as **orange** and **grapefruit**, for an instant pick-me-up.

Thyme, though known for its antibiotic properties, can also fight off negative vibes and give an instant boost to your mood.

WAXING MOON

Clear and cleanse the mind and spirit, and nourish and restore your soul so you may focus on the job at hand. Cleansing and confidence-boosting essential oils include:

Common sage, is good for cleansing rituals and easing mental fatigue.

Lemon, which offers a fresh, clean, energizing boost.

Lime, cheerful and fresh, is said to cleanse, purify, and renew the spirit.

Peppermint, with its familiar uplifting, stimulating aroma, has a cooling effect on the body that can help ease aches and pains.

Rosemary, with a stimulating, invigorating aroma that can help improve memory and stimulate circulation, leaving you ready to take on the world, or at least your small part of it!

Spearmint, a somewhat softer aroma than peppermint, this can help ease headaches and stress. Match peppermint and spearmint's refreshing qualities to your intentions relating to new ideas.

Virginian cedarwood, which smells of the woods, can help calm anxiety and nervous tension and increase focus.

FULL MOON

Let go of negative emotions and dispel distraction to feel balanced, focused, and centered. This is also a time to celebrate and give thanks. Balancing and grounding essential oils include:

Frankincense, which comes from the tree resin and has been used since ancient times for numerous purposes, but is most often associated with spiritual work. Its sweet, fresh, somewhat spicy aroma can calm and relax. As one of the three gifts of the Magi, it is symbolic of worship, honor, and giving thanks.

Orange, zesty, fragrant, and uplifting, it lends a cheerful note of celebration.

Patchouli, best described as earthy, is not for everyone, but it can aid in meditating and focusing intentions.

Sandalwood, with its sweet, woody aroma, which is deeply grounding with the ability to instill inner peace.

Virginian cedarwood, which is also good to use for this phase; see Waxing Moon (page 83) for other uses.

WANING MOON

Relax, slow down, open your mind and heart, and boost your intuition, making you receptive to Nature's messages and signals; this is a time of forgiveness and letting go. Relaxing, healing essential oils include:

Clary sage, herbaceous, floral, and slight fruity, this can help calm the nerves and open your paths of natural intuition.

Geranium, it has a strong floral scent that may require some adjusting to, but it is calming in small quantities.

Lavender, a perennial favorite, which is usually first to mind when we need to de-stress and relax, and even drift off to sleep.

Roman chamomile's bright, crisp scent, which is helpful in letting go of stress and anger. Like lavender, Roman chamomile can help promote sleep.

Rose, the oil's fragrant properties are said to calm and heal.

Ylang-ylang, with its delicate, slightly fruity-floral aroma, which can help boost creativity, ease stress, and diffuse anger.

CAUTION

—

Essential oils can be particularly strong. Carefully read labels regarding their safe use and precautions. Not all oils are safe for bodily use—or even the same quality from brand to brand. They can cause irritation or allergic reactions, or even be toxic.

If using oils on your body, test a small area first to ensure there is no adverse reaction and stick to the feet, arms, and legs, avoiding the genitals and the face completely.

Never ingest an essential oil.

Do not use on damaged skin or on young children, pregnant people, pets, or the elderly, who may be sensitive to the oils' properties.

CANDLES
AND MOON MAGIC

Candles, being man-made, do not have the same innate vibrational energy as natural herbs, oils, or gems (beeswax or soy candles may be slightly more energized due to their natural origins). But when you understand a color's particular corresponding energy levels, you can use the same color candle to enhance your intention setting, which is the best use for candles in your Moon magic routine.

Sunlight comprises all colors of the spectrum, which can be separated with a prism into a rainbow of individual colors. Each color that makes up sunlight represents a different energy level/frequency/vibration and, as we saw with crystals, frequencies affect us variously—and individually. Candle magic also tells us that specific candles may be used on specific days of the week, because their colors are also associated with different celestial objects.

While one candle's wax may be differently colored from the next, each color, no matter red, green, black, etc., burns the same color light. So, you may want to consider using natural-colored candles placed in various colored votives or holders—or even holders made from a particular crystal or gemstone—or focus on the candlelight itself, symbolizing the Moon's fullest light, to absorb its energies based on your goals.

Following is a quick guide to candle colors and their meanings to help you further your Moon magic vibes.

BLACK

Significance: Protection from negative energy
**Corresponding Day/Celestial Object for
Additional Energy:** Saturday (Saturn)

BLUE AND DEEP BLUE

Significance: Meditation, tranquility, patience,
kindness, sincerity
**Corresponding Day/Celestial Object for
Additional Energy:** Thursday (Jupiter)

GREEN

Significance: Growth, money, fertility, good
luck, abundance, renewal, success
**Corresponding Day/Celestial Object for
Additional Energy:** Friday (Venus)

LAVENDER

Significance: Intuition, peace, spiritual growth,
protection
**Corresponding Day/Celestial Object for
Additional Energy:** All

ORANGE AND GOLD

Significance: Joy, energy, fertility, creativity,
changing luck, attraction, stimulation
**Corresponding Day/Celestial Object for
Additional Energy:** Sunday (the Sun)

PURPLE

Significance: Spiritual awareness, wisdom
**Corresponding Day/Celestial Object for
Additional Energy:** Wednesday (Mercury)

RED AND DEEP RED

Significance: Passion, energy, love, power, courage
**Corresponding Day/Celestial Object for
Additional Energy:** Tuesday (Mars)

ROSE AND PINK

Significance: Love, friendship, harmony, joy,
faith, forgiveness
**Corresponding Day/Celestial Object for
Additional Energy:** All

WHITE, SILVER, AND GRAY

Significance: Cleansing, peace, truth,
clairvoyance
**Corresponding Day/Celestial Object for
Additional Energy:** Monday (the Moon)

YELLOW

Significance: Personal power and self-esteem;
realizing and manifesting thoughts, confidence,
creativity, mental clarity, intuition
**Corresponding Day/Celestial Object for
Additional Energy:** Sunday (the Sun)

THE MOON,
ASTROLOGY,

— AND —

TAROT

O ur ancestors have looked to the sky to explain the unknown for millennia. Combining elements of the magical and mystical with a bit of science, astrology is the ages-old study of the stars and planets—and their movement and positions in the sky—to determine their influences on your life. Practicing astrologers refer to the twelve signs of the Zodiac as a basis for divining your future and predicting your horoscope.

Each Zodiac sign is also rooted in Nature, and is assigned one of its elements—fire, water, air, and earth—to reveal even more about your personality.

Likewise, today's tarot, though only several centuries old and believed to have originated in Italy around 1300 CE as a simple card game, combines facets of astrology, Nature, and lots of self-awareness—with nothing evil or dark magical about it—to form a (surprisingly!) accurate picture of where you've been and where you're headed. The most popular deck used today, the Rider-Waite deck, combines varied religious principles, astrological symbols, and Nature's elements.

Let's consider both astrology and tarot in relation to the Moon's phases as we pursue a magical peek into our daily lives.

ASTROLOGICAL SIGNS

Each sign corresponds to a birth month and contains traits that define your personality; these signs can help you understand which parts you show to the world and use to their fullest, as well as those you manage carefully to stay on track. Most people are at least acquainted with their Sun, or "star sign," based on their birth date and birth month. Not sure? Check pages 96 to 99.

Your zodiac sign is associated with certain personality characteristics. And if your sign is designated a fire or an air sign, you generally tend toward positive/extroverted (masculine) tendencies; water and earth signs are the opposite—receptive/subtle (feminine).

As the Full Moon reoccurs throughout the year, traveling through each sign, those traits associated with each sign are amplified—and felt by those whose intuition is attuned enough to notice. The following offers a snapshot of each sign's significant traits—the good and not so good. Find yours and consider, during the next Full Moon, which traits will be on full display, as well as those that may need, well, a little extra management to help you stay in the moment and live your best purposeful life. Set your intentions accordingly and open yourself to the power of the Full Moon.

THE MOON'S PHASES
AND YOUR HOROSCOPE

As we've seen, the eight phases of the Moon are a complete cycle, each with its own energy. There are *active phases*, times to set intentions, make choices, and accomplish goals, and *reflective, or receptive, phases*, times of reduced energy, reflection, and adjusting.

THE MOON'S ACTIVE PHASES

* New
* First Quarter
* Full Moon
* Last (Third) Quarter

THE MOON'S REFLECTIVE PHASES

* Waxing Crescent
* Waxing Gibbous
* Waning Gibbous
* Waning Crescent (or Balsamic)

Keep in mind the general personality characteristics of your birth sign. As the Moon travels through each of its eight phases, you'll feel its influence on your horoscope accordingly.

ESSENTIAL OILS AND THE ZODIAC

Essential oils in your Moon rituals can cleanse a space, heighten the senses, and tame negative energies. Each Zodiac sign also has a particular affinity with an essential oil, see pages 96 to 99, to help you focus your Moon magic, should you choose to use it. This oil might be a particularly good one to start with, but don't limit yourself—have fun experimenting with as many as you like. Some research on an individual oil's properties and your sign's traits can lead to more creative pairings.

NEW MOON

Being an active phase, this dark period is all about discovery. The picture is not fully illuminated, so pay attention to new information received in all formats, including your intuition. Ask questions, of others and yourself. Take opportunities to engage in your favorite activities and take time to be thoughtful and reflect on your goals and intentions. This is a great time to begin something new.

WAXING CRESCENT

The Moon's growing light corresponds to your growing determination to meet goals and challenges. It is a time to commit to what you can achieve, but to do so means knowing fully why your goal is important. Let your intuition guide you and do not be deterred by challenges. Seek information in unusual places.

FIRST QUARTER MOON

Another active phase, this is a great time to look forward and let the past go. Don't hold a grudge; do something to help others and you'll help yourself at the same time. You have what it takes to manifest your intentions. Reflect on your plan and move forward with bold actions.

WAXING GIBBOUS

Whatever your plan, this is the phase devoted to analyzing and refining it. Those questions you've asked, those actions you've taken—how are they working? With your eyes on the prize, clear the path and continue your progress. It may be hard, but trust your instincts and know that you, alone, have what it takes. Utilize your analytical skills for problem solving.

FULL MOON

The full light of this Moon shows everything—no more shadows, no more doubt. It is the chance to see things in full clarity. This is your time to rely on the collective strength of others to help you achieve what you've been working toward—or see clearly what's not working and begin to think about the next New Moon. Congratulate yourself for all you have done and make plans with a friend to celebrate. You will learn things from others that shape how you view the future.

WANING GIBBOUS

As the Moon passes into this dimming phase, it is time, again, for reflection. Feelings and emotions emerge when you reflect on what you have learned since the start of the cycle. Share your insights for the benefit of others. Physical activity and group events are good for your body, mind, and soul.

LAST (THIRD) QUARTER

This last active phase is one of responsibility. Recognize your missteps and shift your thinking to align. This is your last chance, in this cycle, to push forward to achieve your goals—before the Moon's light fades. Now is a time to make amends, tie up loose ends, and spend some energy on self-care.

WANING CRESCENT

This time of reflection challenges your senses other than sight. In the darkened sky, the Moon's energy stimulates them. Listen to music! Indulge in a special meal. Meditate. Get a massage . . . take action to renew your energies as the Moon enters a new cycle. Take time to be still and rest. Listen to your heart and prepare for a new beginning.

ARIES

March 21–
April 20

THE RAM: FIRE SIGN

Let Shine in the Full Moon's Glow: Courage,
determination, confidence
Allow to Dim as the Moon's Light Sets:
Impatience, moodiness, aggressiveness
Associated Essential Oil: Rosemary—a strongly
scented oil as strong as you are, helping you
stay focused and supporting confidence, while
battling impatience and moodiness.

TAURUS

April 21–May 21

THE BULL: EARTH SIGN

Let Shine in the Full Moon's Glow: Reliability,
patience, practicality
Allow to Dim as the Moon's Light Sets:
Stubbornness, possessiveness, uncompromising
Associated Essential Oil: Rose—softens some of
those "strong as a bull" tendencies; eases stress.

GEMINI

May 22–
June 21

THE TWINS: AIR SIGN

Let Shine in the Full Moon's Glow:
Friendliness, gentleness, charm, curiosity
Allow to Dim as the Moon's Light Sets:
Nervousness, inconsistency, indecision
Associated Essential Oil: Basil—supports
your dual nature by stimulating the mind,
encouraging your natural curiosity, and
counterbalancing any indecisiveness.

THE CRAB: WATER SIGN

Let Shine in the Full Moon's Glow: Nurturing, bravery, loyalty

Allow to Dim as the Moon's Light Sets: Moodiness, defensiveness, insecurity

Associated Essential Oil: German (blue) chamomile—supports your nurturing qualities and offsets any natural moodiness.

CANCER
June 22–
July 22

THE LION: FIRE SIGN

Let Shine in the Full Moon's Glow: Pride, creativity, warm-heartedness

Allow to Dim as the Moon's Light Sets: Arrogance, stubbornness, inflexibility

Associated Essential Oil: Jasmine—Leo's natural pride—and stubbornness—may lead to feelings of exhaustion and depression, which jasmine's exotic fragrance can lift.

LEO
July 23–
August 22

THE MAIDEN: EARTH SIGN

Let Shine in the Full Moon's Glow: Analytical, insightful, productive

Allow to Dim as the Moon's Light Sets: Critical, anxious, no fun

Associated Essential Oil: Lavender—promotes a sense of calm and peace, heightening your natural intuition and relieving stress and anxiety.

VIRGO
August 23–
September 23

LIBRA

September 24–
October 23

THE SCALES: AIR SIGN
Let Shine in the Full Moon's Glow:
Cooperation, fair-mindedness, graciousness
Allow to Dim as the Moon's Light Sets:
Indecision, frivolous, superficiality
Associated Essential Oil: Geranium—like
the sign of the scales, this oil is calming and
balancing, helping restore equilibrium and ease
fear and depression.

SCORPIO

October 24–
November 22

THE SCORPION: WATER SIGN
Let Shine in the Full Moon's Glow: Passion,
bravery, resiliency
Allow to Dim as the Moon's Light Sets:
Emotional, jealously, secrecy
Associated Essential Oil: Patchouli—if that
naturally sensual side is feeling a bit sidelined,
turn to patchouli to get you back in the game;
also eases stress that may result from your
sometimes-stinging nature.

SAGITTARIUS

November 23–
December 21

THE CENTAUR: FIRE SIGN
Let Shine in the Full Moon's Glow:
Adventurousness, generosity, intelligence
Allow to Dim as the Moon's Light Sets:
Impatience, rudeness, overpromises
Associated Essential Oil: Black pepper (best
used as part of a blend)—helps keep you alert
and on your toes.

THE MOUNTAIN GOAT: EARTH SIGN   CAPRICORN

December 22–
January 20

Let Shine in the Full Moon's Glow: Discipline, leadership, analytical
Allow to Dim as the Moon's Light Sets: Selfishness, condescension, know-it-all
Associated Essential Oil: Vetiver—sometimes a natural-born leader just needs to relax, unwind, and be soothed.

THE WATER BEARER: AIR SIGN   AQUARIUS

January 21–
February 19

Let Shine in the Full Moon's Glow: Generosity, humanity, tolerance, perceptiveness
Allow to Dim as the Moon's Light Sets: Temperamental, inability to compromise, aloof
Associated Essential Oil: Neroli—despite your natural humanity, you sometimes feel alone, leading to stress and depression; neroli's intense fragrance helps promote sleep and eases stress, putting you back in the swim again.

THE FISH: WATER SIGN   PISCES

February 20–
March 20

Let Shine in the Full Moon's Glow: Dreamer, compassion, artistic, intuitive
Allow to Dim as the Moon's Light Sets: Worry, indecision, overly trusting
Associated Essential Oil: Melissa—creative types are also emotional types and Melissa can help balance the extremes, while supporting your natural compassion and intuition.

YOUR SIGN AND A LUNAR ECLIPSE

Remember, lunar eclipses (see page 35) usually signify change, and change can be uncomfortable. A lunar eclipse does not have to fall in your sign to affect you, but if the lunar eclipse presents during that time, consider the following:

Aries: As the first sign of the Zodiac, a lunar eclipse can signify an especially good time for a change. Your confidence and creativity are at peak levels to accept the challenge. Take action, but be patient for results.

Taurus: Taurus is stubborn. A lunar eclipse is a sure sign of impending change that can shake your confidence, but your practical, patient qualities enable you to embrace and define the change to your benefit.

Gemini: Your friendliness and charm ensure the changes signified by an eclipse are nothing but smooth sailing. Put your tendency toward indecision aside and move forward with confident strides. Make those changes you've been dreaming about and feel a renewed energy for life.

Cancer: Accentuate your loyal, nurturing tendencies to care for relationships at this time. Let these relationships boost your confidence to tackle anything you've been putting off.

Leo: Leos can carry a grudge. Now is the time to tap into your cooperative, gracious side and wipe the slate clean. Let go of bad habits and write down the positive actions you will replace them with.

Virgo: The darkness of the eclipse can trigger contemplation and inward reflection. Know this is a time to let your brave warrior shine, to implement change for the better.

Libra: This time of change will lead you to new adventures. Seek people and places you've been meaning to visit. Put an end to procrastination.

Scorpio: Your analytical nature may have you rethinking old problems. Take action to correct any past mistakes and tidy up your life. Now is a great time to end bad habits.

Sagittarius: Your creativity is at its highest and you're open to new challenges. Feel confident walking a new path.

Capricorn: You are hardworking and loyal. Look for those qualities to be rewarded during an eclipse with reciprocated help and some fun, new opportunities.

Aquarius: Your generosity is on display during this time. Expect to gain in greater amounts than you give. Some compromise may be required to navigate the change this time brings.

Pisces: You're both a dreamer and a worrier. Use this time to take care of yourself to be able to weather the change.

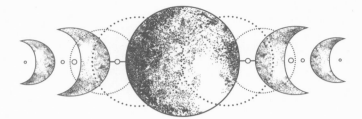

MOON SIGNS

Moon signs, versus Sun signs, are not about those observable personality traits, but rather reflect your inner self, thoughts, feelings, fears, and emotions . . . even those unknown to you. This sign is more difficult to calculate because the Moon moves through the Zodiac quickly (visiting each sign for only two to three days). However, as the Moon moves through the Zodiac and appears in your sign, she provides a clue as to how you'll likely react to life and its inevitable ups and downs. Here's a quick list for reference.

The Moon in . . .

Aries: Initial excitement for anything new, followed by waning interest.

Taurus: Sensitive and affectionate—and not afraid to show it.

Gemini: Dual nature adapts and changes as needed.

Cancer: Kind and sensitive . . . maybe a bit too much.

Leo: The dramatist—try to keep it to yourself.

Virgo: Extremely artistic and sensitive, but prone to overanalyzing your feelings.

Libra: Quite charming, and able to correctly size up any situation for the best decision.

Scorpio: Compassionate and intuitive, but likes things even-keeled.

Sagittarius: Sensitive to others' feelings.

Capricorn: You keep emotions bottled up, and it's not good for you.

Aquarius: Tend to reflect the feelings/emotions of others around you.

Pisces: Sensitive to others' emotions.

You can find numerous online Moon sign calculators, if you'd like to explore this notion in more detail.

One Zodiac sign, in particular, is ruled by the Moon—that's Cancer—and it is the only sign paid a visit by its ruler every month. Being born a Cancer means being security obsessed. You're a homebody, but also fearless enough to create your secure place in the world.

Whether born a Cancer or not, take advantage of the Full Moon in Cancer to summon the brave warrior in you to tackle any problems currently in your way and return that sense of peace and security to your world.

A warrior is not discouraged, does not give up the fight.
Great Moon, with courage, I state my choice, to carry on with might.
A smiling face will be my mask to hide my fear and doubt,
And all will see the strength in me grow braver by the night.

So, whether water, fire, air, earth, Sun, or Moon sign, join forces with the Moon's energies to celebrate what makes you, *you*!

THE MOON AND TAROT

"Tarot" is any of a set, usually, of seventy-eight, playing cards including twenty-two pictorial cards used for fortune-telling. While one could say a fortune-teller "reads your future" in the cards, I would say they read your current circumstances and the pictorial representations heighten both our intuition and awareness. Once we are aware, we can be conscious about making things happen or taking advantage of circumstances to our benefit—it's like that new car you just bought that you now see everyone else driving . . . no, not everyone bought that same new car at the same time as you, but you are certainly hyperaware enough of your new circumstances to notice similarities everywhere (or maybe subconsciously seek them out). I think of tarot the same way—heightening your intuition and sense of awareness based on what the cards tell you or your reader.

The Moon and tarot align as superpowers to enhance that awareness . . . made real by your intention setting and intuition of what the cards are telling you.

TAROT DECK

It wasn't until around 1700 that a tarot deck, similar to what we know today, was created. Eliphas Levi, a Catholic priest and teacher, devised it, saying it helped his students along their paths to spiritual enlightenment and self-awareness. Today's most popular deck, the beautifully illustrated Rider-Waite deck, created in 1909, is built upon Levi's work but in recognition that the deck can be more powerful than just enhancing self-awareness—it could actually help foresee the future.

A typical tarot deck is divided into the Major Arcana and Minor Arcana. The Major Arcana comprises the twenty-two picture cards, which tell a tale of your journey, beginning with the Fool and ending with the World, when the journey begins anew, reminiscent of the Moon's phases and cycles.

The Minor Arcana are the forty numbered suit cards (like a regular playing deck), whose four suits, each numbered 1 through 10, equal Cups, Swords, Pentacles, and Wands. Each suit corresponds to one of Nature's elements, and these cards are like the details of your journey in what they reveal:

* Cups = water (relationships and emotional issues)
* Swords = air (communication and intellectual matters)
* Pentacles = earth (all things material)
* Wands = fire (life's passion and creativity)

The Minor Arcana also include the sixteen Court cards—kings, queens, knights, and pages—that represent the people of the tarot, but let's leave those for another time.

THE MOON CARD

———

The seventy-eight–card tarot deck includes a Moon card among the Major Arcana. It is the eighteenth card. While the Moon illuminates, her light——not as bright as the Sun's——also creates shadows. This is the Moon card . . . lighting a path not fully seen——one dependent on intuition and your subconscious to navigate. Be aware of the unknown, but also open to the light the Moon shines on all that you imagine in life.

THE MAJOR ARCANA
AND THE MOON

You don't have to wait for any certain phase of the Moon to work with
your tarot deck or have a reading, but the energy surrounding the Moon
at that time can certainly influence how you perceive the information
and what you do with it. It's often said it's best to time a reading based
on the type of question you have. For example, looking to grow your
business? The Waxing Gibbous Moon may be your best time to explore
this, as she grows to Full Moonness and offers her wisdom and energy.
Feel like ending a relationship is on the horizon? Consider a reading
during the Waning Moon as a prime time to take on this question.

Additionally, each Major Arcana tarot card has an association with a
Moon phase. Understanding the card's meaning and connecting it with
a lunar phase can help you be in the moment and realize the possibilities.

NEW MOON

Major Arcana Tarot Card: The Fool
Message: Take a risk. Have some fun. Feel the
energy of something new about to begin. View the
world through the eyes of a child.

CRESCENT MOON

Major Arcana Tarot Card: The High Priestess
Message: Honor new beginnings. Nurture
what's important. Embrace the day by living fully
and intentionally.

FIRST QUARTER MOON

Major Arcana Tarot Card: The Magician
Message: Create a little magic: make someone's
dream come true, no matter the size. Make the
impossible seem easy. Set a goal.

GIBBOUS MOON

Major Arcana Tarot Card: The Wheel of Fortune
Message: Grow yourself: learn something new.
Try new activities. Meet new people.

FULL MOON

Major Arcana Tarot Cards: The Sun; The Moon
Message: Acknowledge the abundance in your life.
Share your bounty (knowledge, time, money) with
others. Shine friendship's warm light on others who
need help.

WANING GIBBOUS MOON

Major Arcana Tarot Card: The Star
Message: Stop. Breathe. Take in your
surroundings. Reflect on lessons learned. Take
time to connect with others. Offer to help.

LAST QUARTER MOON

Major Arcana Tarot Card: Judgement
Message: Reflect on past experiences, while
considering future action. Attend to unfinished
business. Follow the plan.

WANING CRESCENT

Major Arcana Tarot Card: The Hermit
Message: Seek your inner wisdom. Attend to your
health. Rest. Let go.

THE MAJOR ARCANA
AND THE ZODIAC

Finally, specific Major Arcana tarot cards can also be linked to each Zodiac sign, providing further insight into the essence of one's persona. Consider these revelations when layering on the Moon's magical messages.

THE EMPEROR

Linked Zodiac Symbol: Aries
Personality Revealed: Loyal, royal, and dependable.

THE HIEROPHANT

Linked Zodiac Symbol: Taurus
Personality Revealed: Seek mentors to expand knowledge and insights.

THE LOVERS

Linked Zodiac Symbol: Gemini
Personality Revealed: Exposes the dual personality of Gemini and the choices this split often presents.

THE CHARIOT

Linked Zodiac Symbol: Cancer
Personality Revealed: Intuitive and proud,
you steer a steady course.

STRENGTH

Linked Zodiac Symbol: Leo
Personality Revealed: You have the courage to
overcome any obstacles that may come your way.

THE HERMIT

Linked Zodiac Symbol: Virgo
Personality Revealed: You need your "me" time
to recharge.

JUSTICE

Linked Zodiac Symbol: Libra
Personality Revealed: Objective and fair-minded.

DEATH

Linked Zodiac Symbol: Scorpio
Personality Revealed: Slightly mysterious, Death signals rebirth and the ability to change and adapt as needed.

TEMPERANCE

Linked Zodiac Symbol: Sagittarius
Personality Revealed: Able to navigate any storm in a clear-headed manner, you are a negotiator par excellence.

THE DEVIL

Linked Zodiac Symbol: Capricorn
Personality Revealed: Don't fear the shadows.
See what hides there so you may conquer fears
and emerge confident and strong.

THE STAR

Linked Zodiac Symbol: Aquarius
Personality Revealed: Reach for the stars; you
know you'll get there.

THE MOON

Linked Zodiac Symbol: Pisces
Personality Revealed: Ruled by ever-changing
moods, you are in rhythm with Nature's cycles;
intuitive and compassionate.

WORKING YOUR MOON MAGIC

WITH

SIMPLE RITUALS AND SPELLS

Now that you've learned all about the Moon's energy and phases, discovered various tools to help you harness her magic, and practiced a few bits of Moon magic yourself, it's time to strike out on your own—to unleash your inner Moon goddess and use her energy and charms to help manifest your intentions and live the most magical life yet.

Here we'll explore some rituals and spells to get you started. Remember, it's all about your intentions and using the Moon's various phases to amplify the energies needed or that are present to bring about change.

Keep in mind, as with any skill, you'll need to practice, but believe in the power of you—your unique energy and vibration. When you link that amazing power to other positive energies in the Universe, great things can happen. Blessed be.

RITUALS

Rituals, as old as time, are ceremonial acts or observances. Our Moon magic rituals mark an occasion—one of celebration, or contemplation, or healing, or joy—for whatever your life needs or wants at that particular moment. It is a chance for you to express your gratitude, request help, or just generally explore the Moon's magical energies and phases through intention setting and intentional living. The rituals here can get you on your way. As your confidence builds, create some of your own, with special meaning to you.

SMUDGING

Smudging is a Native American ritual that closely traces its origins to burning incense, which is a ritual that can be traced back to ancient Egypt, where it was used in religious ceremonies and to ward off evil.

Smudging is the act of burning a natural substance for a specific reason, historically for cleansing, healing, and spiritual purposes. In the Moon magical sense, you can incorporate it into any ritual you like to clear negative energy and increase the focus on intention setting, or simply do it alone to help resolve a time when you are feeling particularly sad or "stuck." Some people do it seasonally; some weekly. You do you.

There are four common herbs used for smudging, with sage being the most common:

* Sage, for healing and dispelling negativity
* Lavender, for restoring balance and peace
* Cedar, for purifying and attracting positive energy
* Sweetgrass, for blessing

SMUDGING RITUAL

Smudging should not be rushed—give yourself at least fifteen minutes, or the time to practice this intentionally, with a focus on the reason or desired outcome. Add the power of smudging to any Moon ritual you like, or offer it in preparation for another ritual.

    Note: Make sure the area(s) you're smudging are well ventilated so the negativity flows out and the positivity flows in. Do not include infants, the elderly, pregnant women, or anyone with respiratory issues in the process when burning herbs. And take care and precautions with flames, as always.

On a table, gather the following:

* Candle and matches
* Smudge stick, purchase one online or make your own herb bundle (see page 116 for typical herbs used)
* Heatproof bowl, for placing under the smudge stick as it smolders, ensuring no embers or other hot materials land anywhere they shouldn't
* Additional heatproof bowl, containing sand, salt, or other material to extinguish the smudge stick
* Journal and pen (optional)
* Care and common sense

1. Be still for a moment. Focus on your intent and believe it will manifest: It can be anything you feel you need at this time—becoming unstuck (releasing negative energy), generating creativity, dispelling sadness, blessing a new home, or becoming focused and centered. Be aware of your breathing as you focus.

2. Light the candle with the matches.

3. Light the smudge stick with the candle flame. Holding it over the heatproof bowl, gently fan the smudge stick to extinguish its flame; you want it to smoke/smolder, not burn.

4. To cleanse your space, begin at the doorway to the room or house and gently wave the smudge stick around the perimeter of the space, paying special attention to corners, where negative energies can congregate. The smoke will absorb the negative energy and cleanse the space, taking it away as it flows out the window. Slowly move into the center of the room, fanning the smoke up and out of the open windows. You may want to repeat your intentions while doing this, or just focus on the process. Visualize the smoke carrying away anything negative.

5. When finished, extinguish the smudge stick in the bowl of sand, making sure it is completely out before leaving it unattended.

6. Take a moment to give thanks to the herbs for their power and continue on with your Moon ritual, as desired, or journal your thoughts at this time.

SMUDGING SPRAY

If you're hesitant about burning things inside your home, or you just object to the smoke (for any reason), making your own smudging spray is easy and convenient, and can bring the same cleansing and clearing effect you need. Using an essential oil—in this case, sage—means you have the same herbal healing properties as with the plant. Use this for a specific purpose, such as blessing a new home/space (see page 144) or any time you feel stuck or as though negative energies are weighing you down.

You only need a few simple tools: an 8-ounce (240 ml) glass spray bottle (dark glass, if possible), ¾ cup (180 ml) of Moon water (see page 125), sage essential oil, 2 tablespoons (30 ml) vodka, Himalayan salt, and a small clear quartz crystal (to supercharge the water with its energy).

The Moon's waning phase is the best time to coordinate this release of negative energy, but use the spray any time you feel the need.

1. In the bottle, combine ½ cup (120 ml) of Moon water, 10 to 15 drops of sage essential oil, the vodka (it helps disperse the oil in the water, as they otherwise won't mix), and a large pinch of salt (to help absorb any negative energies).
2. Add the remaining ¼ cup (60 ml) of Moon water and the crystal. Cap the bottle and shake to combine, and do this again before each use.
3. Spray lightly around yourself, avoiding the face and eyes, or around a room, or the entire space—and no burning means more smudging opportunities (think: office, hotel room, car).
4. It's helpful to invoke a prayer or mantra during this ritual.

Water and oil, cleanse this space, filling it with light and grace.
The negative is banished here, where thankfully, and blessed be,
We feel your warm embrace.

MOON CIRCLE

Your circle is your sacred space. It can be made with physical objects, such as crystals or stones, or can simply be drawn with your finger in the air. It is a place to gather and a place to create energy. It is a powerful place.

Gather your friends under the next Full Moon to connect and amplify their energies by joining hands in a circle, standing or sitting, around an altar you've made (see page 138), if you wish. If desired, each person can place an object to be charged with the Moon's energy inside the circle or on the altar. The purpose of your circle is to celebrate and honor the Goddess Moon and all her gifts, to open yourself to her light, increasing intuition.

Use the circle for intention setting. Create and chant your own mantra to raise the energies around you. Stand or sit silently in meditation on your intentions. Sing or dance clockwise in the circle. Light a candle in memory of someone or something when it's time to bring the circle to a close.

Take a moment to give thanks for the seasonal blessings of the Moon and friends. Walk or dance counterclockwise to dissolve the circle.

Blessed be.

BLUE MOON RITUAL

Take advantage of the beauty and light this special Full Moon offers by performing a ritual to focus your thoughts. It can be as simple or elaborate as you like; this is a very simple ritual.

Clear your space of negative energy and thought—a simple way is to burn some fresh sage (see page 117) to clear the negativity and open a window to let it flow out of your space. Or tidy the space and spray a favorite scent or diffuse an essential oil . . . anything that gives you a feeling of freshness.

Light a candle to set the mood; its color (see page 88) or scent (see pages 82 to 85) may depend on your desires to be fulfilled, or use white, or blue, to mirror the Blue Moon's silent energy.

Sit comfortably, outside or in, somewhere you can see the Moon's glow. Close your eyes, or gaze into the candle flame, and breathe deeply, feeling the Moon's pull with each breath in, and releasing any tension or negative thoughts with each breath out.

Concentrate on your intention. Do you want to fill your life with more joy? Do you want to boost self-esteem to be ready to tackle the world? Whatever it is, when you're ready, say quietly or aloud:

I am filled with the Moon's guiding light.
I am filled with joy.
In this light, I see I am strong; I feel safe and loved.
I can live joyfully and I will live purposefully to care for mysel and others.
Thank you for your energy and wisdom, fair Moon.

Let the candle burn down, and take time to reflect on your thoughts or write them in your journal.

MONEY WOES?

Take advantage of the unique power of a Blue Moon to fill yourself with energy and purpose, to refocus.

Go outside and, literally, breathe in the light and energy of the Moon. Having a green jade stone with you will boost your lucky energies and bring opportunities for wealth.

Keep a clear head and focus on the problem to be solved. What will help? Polish the resume; apply for a new job; approach your boss about a raise; set a budget and keep to it?

What will you do to increase your worth, not just monetarily, this month?

When gentle waves of Moonbeams sing,
soft charming songs doth tell,
Of shimmering riches, lo' behold,
there borne upon their wings.

JOYFUL ENERGY

For no other reason than living joyfully, have a Blue Moon dance party (see page 126) and energize yourself to meet life's challenges and recognize its rewards fully in the coming weeks and months.

THE FULL MOON
AND YOUR BIRTH MONTH

If you'd like to incorporate a ritual or two to mark the occasion, consider a Moon bath (see page 126) or create a Moon circle (see page 120). While the Full Moon represents a culmination of sorts, it's also a time to give thanks and be grateful for who we are and all we have.

O' brilliant Moon, your light fills me with warmth, wisdom, and a wealth of energy to walk with purpose and grace on the path before me. It shows me the way to honor those with me on this journey. I will speak with kindness and act with charity. I release any negative thoughts or feelings to make room for my intentions.

What is your intention? How will you use the power of the Full Moon in your sign?

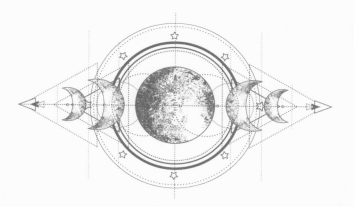

LUNAR ECLIPSE MAGIC: MOON WISHES

Because lunar eclipses occur during Full Moons, they offer a special time to honor change, celebrate growth and healing, and tap into our inner resolve. If you can, stand outside and feel the energy of aligning with the Universe: Sun, Earth, You, and the Moon, all in harmony. Consider a ritual to honor the event and give thanks to the power of Nature to heal. Mark the occasion alone or invite your favorite group of like-minded friends.

1. Pick a location where the Moon is visible. In good weather, being outdoors lets you feel that full connection with Nature and its calming, harmonious, influence.
2. Cleanse the space with a sage smudge (see page 117) or incense.
3. Set an altar (see page 138), if desired, with special objects, crystals, or other natural items.
4. Set the mood: music, candles, comfortable places to sit, and food (and wine) are all great options.
5. Gather paper, pens, and matches (if you need to let go of something), as well as a proper container to burn it in.
6. Take time to meditate on your intentions and then write them down. It's advised that writing down our goals increases the rate of success in achieving them. Share them with the group, if you like. Stating intentions aloud, to others, helps cement our accountability to them.
7. Put your Moon wishes in a special place—under your pillow, in a wish box, or in an intention jar and observe the results.

MOON WATER

During the Moon's Full phase, when her energy is at its height, place a large lidded container outside (yard, balcony, porch) where it can catch the Moon's beams, or place it near a window that receives Moonlight. Fill it with water (use spring or distilled water if you're using it for culinary purposes), cover the container, and let it bathe in the light of the Moon. Take a moment to focus your intentions into the water, then let it infuse with the Moon's nourishing energy.

The next day, the water is ready to use. Label it and keep refrigerated, if you wish. Add the water to your Moon bath, use it to brew Moon Tea, immerse your crystals in it to reenergize them, or just sip as you meditate in the Moon's guiding light.

MOON DANCING

With all that great energy emanating from the Full Moon (the original disco ball in the sky!), now's the time for a dance party. Invite the neighbors or friends for a formalized group event, or keep it simpler—just you. If you're outside, sprinkle some glitter on the grass for a little "mood" magic. Crank up the tunes—or let your inner rhythms guide you—and dance to celebrate life and the culmination of another month's work. Feel the energy cleanse your soul and the joy fill your heart. When finished, take a moment to be quiet and give thanks.

MOON BATHING

In addition to cleansing our bodies, cleansing our psyches is an important part of self-care. Moon bathing is a simple, yet relaxing, soul-cleansing, mind-clearing ritual useful at any phase of the Moon, but is said to be most powerful during a Full Moon, when her purifying energy is at its highest.

Moonlight or water? You do what you prefer and what feels comfortable. If you're lucky enough to live in a warmer climate year-round, bathing in the Moon's light, outside, feeling truly connected to the Earth below your feet and the wondrous stars above, can bring an immense sense of peace. If your luck runs higher and you live near a body of water, a dip in the ocean, river, or lake (even the pool!), can be enormously healing and fulfilling. For everyone else, take advantage of those warmer evenings in summer and fall. No natural water? Use the nearest tub.

MOON BATH RITUAL
BY MOONLIGHT

Prepare a spot in your yard, or a park, porch, or balcony—even near a window; any darkened place you feel safe, connected to Nature, and can touch the Moon's light. Create an altar (see page 138) or offering nearby, if desired, using favorite items such as crystals, candles, incense, photos, or other special objects that relate to your intentions that month and that you'd like to cleanse with the Moon's energy. (Be sure to bring proper holders for any burning objects, along with water and/or a fire-extinguishing product when using flames outdoors.)

Comfortably stand or sit under the Moon's most powerful light, close your eyes, and feel your hands (if sitting) and feet firmly planted to the ground. Breathe. Deeply in. Slowly out. Again. Focus your thoughts on filling your body with the Moon's light and energy on every breath in. With every breath out, feel the energy of your breath and assess the results of your actions this past month. What new insights do they reveal?

MOON BATH RITUAL
IN THE BATHTUB

Prefer the tub? Immersing yourself in water during this phase is another way to feel the pull of the Moon's heightened energy.

Create your magical space, whether with light, music, a journal, etc., and fill your tub with warm water. Add any salts (such as Himalayan) or essential oils you like, or flowers (such as rose petals) or herbs (such as lavender). Place some water-friendly crystals around, or in, the bath, such as rose quartz (unconditional love, compassion, peace), clear quartz (power), seed crystal (wisdom), moonstone, of course (connecting to your inner goddess), or amethyst (protection) to tap into their individual energies.

Step into the tub, immerse yourself, close your eyes, and relax. Feel the water's gentle warmth and softness cradling you and imagine the energy it absorbs from the Moon filling you.

Follow the same breathing ritual as described for bathing in the Moon's light (preceding) and let yourself feel the flow of energy throughout your body.

In either event, stay as long as is comfortable and gently retune to the world around you when finished.

CONNECT WITH THE MOON GODDESSES: GODDESS MEDITATION RITUAL

When your inner Moon goddess feels like she could use a goddess BFF, this simple ritual can help you appeal to the ancient Moon goddesses who came before you. Their wisdom and power are available to get you back on track or boost your confidence to achieve that intention you recently set.

As each goddess can awaken different sacred feminine aspects within, ask for all their gifts, or a specific one, depending on the intentions you've set.

Connecting is simple. Sit in meditation (you can also do this while Moon bathing) and concentrate on the goddess you wish to invite in and any specific area you wish to work on with her. For example, invite Isis to boost your confidence and intuition to tackle a specific situation. When meditating, connect with the goddesses in whatever way resonates with you.

There's nothing more to it than inviting them in and sitting quietly in meditation. Pay attention to your intuitive senses: *clairaudience* (clear healing), *clairsentience* (clear feeling), *claircognizance* (clear knowing), and *clairvoyance* (clear seeing). Depending on which sense is strongest, you may hear, feel, know, or see their guidance, presence, and love.

No matter what, trust that by simply asking for their goddess support you open yourself to connect with your divine feminine gifts, which reveal themselves subtly and mysteriously.

MOON TEA—
NO CAULDRON REQUIRED!

Tea, in many cultures, is a ritual with specific meaning attached. The soothing warmth of a fragrant cup of tea can restore a worried soul. Following the centuries-old traditions of herbal medicine working to heal what ails, you can concoct a batch of Moon tea and drink it daily to refresh your intentions or just incorporate it as part of your Moon rituals and intention setting. Making the tea blends yourself, rather than just buying tea bags, offers a way to slow down and focus on the process. Give thanks to the plants that provide the ingredients for your tea blends and think about how you'll incorporate your tea ritual into intention setting.

To begin, use the Moon water you have on hand or make a batch overnight (see page 125). A general guideline for making teas is to use 2 to 3 teaspoons of a dried herb or herb blend per cup (8 ounces, or 240 ml) of tea. For larger quantities, say a 1-gallon (3.8 L) jar, that translates to about 1 cup (weight varies) of dried herbs.

If you use fresh herbs, those gathered under the Moon's light will be even more inspiring. Place a big handful (a single herb or a mix, grown without pesticides) into a large pot or clean coffeepot. Cover with boiling water and let steep for at least 5 minutes. Close your eyes and inhale the lovely aromas while you take time to meditate, even if for just a few seconds.

When ready to brew your cuppa, boil as much Moon water as needed and steep your tea (in a strainer, tea ball, clean unscented muslin bag, or disposable filter) for about 5 minutes. Sweeten with dried fruits, spices, honey, or dried culinary flowers, like rose petal (rose petal and vanilla are delicious).

LAW OF VIBRATION AND HEALING ENERGY

The law of vibration tells us everything vibrates. And everything in the Universe, being made differently, vibrates at different frequencies. Some of those frequencies are obvious (think: sunlight or music), but some are not. What is obvious, though, is that these energies are all interconnected and influenced by each other, as ripples in a pond.

This simple ritual can send positive energy and vibrations anywhere they're needed.

When something happens that particularly touches you—anywhere in the world—find time in your world to sit quietly, light a candle (any color; any lunar phase), and visualize your good and healing intentions being manifested. Pray for pain to be eased or light to be given. Let the candle burn. Extinguish it. Give thanks to the Universe for your place in it.

ILLUMINATING A PATH IN DARKNESS

This is a particularly good ritual to adopt during the Waning Crescent Moon, as darkness sets in and you reflect on lessons learned and let go of the unproductive. It can help clear negativity from your mind and free you to act in your own best interest.

Gather a sheet of paper, a pen, a heatproof container, and matches.

1. Sitting quietly, take the pen and paper and write out everything you are feeling—uncensored.
2. Do you see any surprises or insights about recurring issues that are important to you? Have you been ignoring or suppressing your feelings in a certain area? Have you been settling, compromising, or dismissing your truth and boundaries? Are you ready to release what's no longer serving you?
3. You don't need to have all the answers, but it's important to ask the questions.

The paper now holds your emotions. To let go of what's bothering you, carefully burn the paper in the heatproof container, while visualizing the smoke carrying the negativity into the skies. Wash away any ashes or surrender them to Mother Earth, and feel the lightness of releasing what ailed.

Take a moment to reflect on what you learned and what you will do to move forward. Create an intention to close the ritual, such as the following. When ready, say quietly or aloud:

I release all that no longer serves me for total healing and purification.
I will walk my path with purpose and gratitude,
for my best and highest good.

LETTING GO

The Waning Crescent Moon is a particularly good time for letting go of things that weigh us down or just don't work in our lives the way they used to. Thank them for their service and create a space in your heart for their help, but say good-bye and move on to something that will be a positive force in your world.

Gather matches, a small sage sprig, paper, a blue or white candle, a pencil, and a small bowl of water.

1. Go to a safe place outside, under the light of the Moon, that holds special meaning for you and light your sage to cleanse your space.
2. Light your candle and express gratitude to the Universe before writing down everything—or a specific thing you need to say good-bye to—that no longer serves.
3. Take a deep breath. Exhale. Read the list quietly or aloud. Breathe in, and, as you exhale, imagine your breath carrying it all away—whatever you want to let go of. Breathe deeply and feel a lightness, an ease, filling the negative space in you.
4. When ready, use the candle to light the paper (safely) and put it in the bowl of water.

Close your ritual by, once again, expressing gratitude.

NEW JOB

If you feel the need for a change in your job or career, setting those intentions during the New Moon can bring powerful results. This two-step ritual starts with a bit of meditation, journaling, and soul searching to clarify intentions. The second step simply harnesses the Moon's energy to get your message out into the Universe. Be open to the vibrations and opportunities around you.

1. Find a quiet, comfortable place in which to think and write. Breathe deeply to calm yourself and focus on your thoughts. What do you need to know? Is it what makes you happy? How to earn more money? To work for a greater good? Let your thoughts work freely on this question. When ready, take pen and paper and write down all the thoughts and ideas that came to you.

2. Next, look for a theme. If there is none, try this: Make three columns—What I Love, What I Can Do, Which Jobs Use These, and fill in the blanks. You may need to come back to this exercise a number of times before you land on the right path for you.

3. When you have a new job or career goal in mind, it's time to tell the world. Under the light of the New Moon, recite this simple spell, quietly or aloud:

With open mind and grateful heart, I ask for your support.
As life brings change, to keep my roots but spread my wings apart.
New job, new goals, new intentions set,
Please help me land the job I'm meant
To bring about the change I seek and flourish from the start.

AND, AWAY GO TROUBLES...

New Moon, Full Moon, and Waning Moon phases are the
most potent for cleansing energies. When you don't have time
for that luxurious Moon bath (see page 126), use this simple
cleansing ritual to meditate your troubles down the drain.

Gather a favorite scented soap (consider an herbal soap
based on your intentions) that is safe for use on hands and face
and a soft towel.

Find a time when distractions are minimized. Take a
moment to focus your intentions on what you'd like to rid from
your world. Have the tap water in your bathroom sink running
at the perfect temperature. Gently wash your hands and face
with the soap, taking time to acknowledge the soothing scent
and give gratitude for the clean water, and then rinse your face
and hands while silently visualizing any troubles being washed
away. Lather, rinse, and repeat as often as needed!

SIMPLE SPELLS
FOR EVERYDAY LIVING

COME, SIT A SPELL; LET'S TALK SPELLS.

Like ancient rituals and religious rites, magic spells (and hexes!) go back centuries, though magic seems to diverge from religion in the way it perceived the gods: religious ceremonies were an act of appeasement—a time to plead with the gods to look favorably upon you; magic spells—and curses—work to utilize a god's particular power to ensure a specific outcome: like winning the next chariot race, or marrying well and happily. Here we'll use the Moon's magical energies, combined with any other tools you desire, such as crystals, candles, goddess power, herbs, and paper and pen.

Casting a spell is to effect an outcome by setting an intention and performing a ritual around it to amplify positive energy. In this book, we only use spells for good. No dark magic here. Your best outcomes will be to focus on you; spells cannot be used to control others. As with intention setting, casting a spell is another way for you to focus your thoughts and effect desired change, coming from a place of peace and light.

As with intention setting and any Moon celebration ritual you choose, make it yours. It can be formal or not, alone or with a group, organized or inspired.

As we've learned, the most powerfully energetic phase of the Moon is its fullest phase. Utilize the Full Moon phase for those particularly trying problems that need a little extra spellbinding boost. Otherwise, any phase of the Moon can be matched to your desires for spell work.

Remember, it's all about the energy. Your spells will be more powerful as you learn to work with the energies the Universe provides. Your thoughts and ideas also have energy, creating their own cosmic vibrations. Releasing them into the Universe with positive intent is thought to bring them back to you threefold. Learning to harness these energies in your spell work, as with intention setting, will bring your desires—but, again, they must be pure and true.

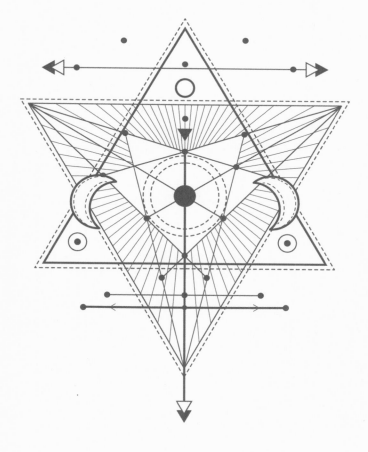

ALTARS

———

An altar does not have to be fancy, and can be as simple as a windowsill or shoebox (to go!). It is a space used as a visual reminder and a place to focus your energy when working in groups, meditating alone, or trying out a spell or two. It can even be a shelf where you display your crystals, candles, or other reminders of your intentions so you are aware of the work you're doing every day.

You may even decide to have more than one altar—each fulfilling a different purpose. Consider an altar by your bed with objects devoted to ease and relaxation. Or one in your work area, helping to boost creativity and energy. Maybe you'll create one dedicated to a sacred Moon goddess or your ancestors. Be as fancy, creative, or minimalist as you like. As much as possible, keep the elements that make up your altar natural, for their innate individual energies.

Physically cleaning the space where your altar resides removes negative energy and makes space for those good vibes to live. Cover your altar with a cloth, if you wish—maybe something that represents your intentions. Try silk for money spells, green for luck, white for ease of mind and focus, or any color that energizes you if you need a boost.

Your altar represents you—your heart, hopes, dreams, intentions, and life. If you stay true to those things, it should be ready to help you work your magic.

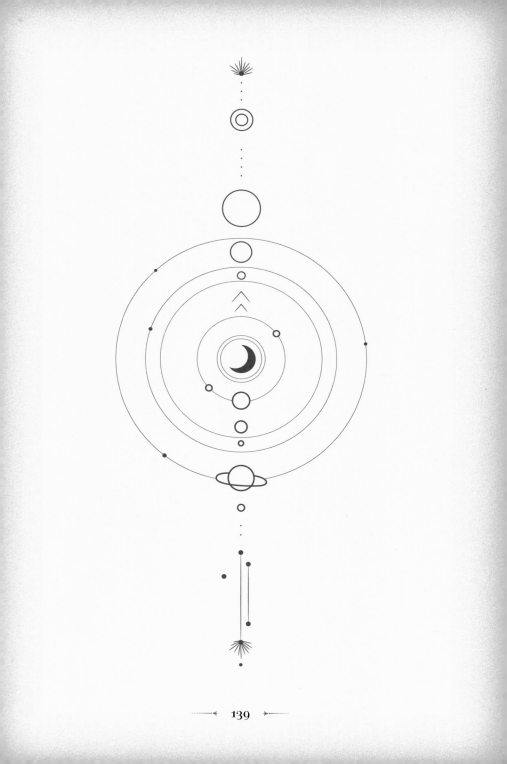

NEW MOON
SPELLS

CLEANSING,
INTENTION SETTING,
NEW BEGINNINGS

MONEY LUCK

The New Moon is a good time for new beginnings or setting the wheels in motion, so try this simple spell for increased earnings, if that is your desire.

In the laws of the Universe, getting more starts with giving more, and giving starts with gratitude. First give thanks for what you have. Take a moment to reflect and set an intention to share your wealth—be it money or talents—with the Universe.

My simple wealth is made of happiness, love, and health. I have talents to share to help others. I will make time to give back to the Universe.

Once you've aligned yourself with gratitude, cast this simple spell.

1. Gather a few pennies in your hand.
2. Go outside, if you can, and stand under the Moon, absorbing its cleansing energy. Feel yourself letting go of any blocking negativity with each breath out. Open your mind to new opportunities with each breath in. Light a candle, if you wish: white or silver works best. Visualize the wealth you desire.
3. When ready, say quietly or aloud:

New Moon, new truth, new time, increase my wealth from pennies to dimes. Increase my value to others, I pray that life grows richer and fuller each day.

4. Take a moment to give thanks to the New Moon's growing wisdom. Bury the pennies in the ground, if you are able, or tuck them away in a dark space and leave them there.

CONQUERING CHANGE

New beginnings are times of change, and times of change can shake even the most confident of us. To help, try this spell during the next Black Moon (or New Moon) phase.

1. Gather a yellow candle and a tiger's eye crystal.
2. Sit quietly, somewhere comfortable, place the candle on a heatproof surface, light it, and imagine yourself acting with confidence and purpose.
3. Take the tiger's eye in your dominant hand. Focusing on the flame, feel it illuminate your soul.
4. Calling on the Black Moon's quiet power, say quietly or aloud:

O' quiet Moon, guide my thoughts,
as I cast aside my fears and doubts.
Fill me instead with peace and resolve,
as I feel my confidence grow and evolve.
This tiger's eye I have in hand,
reminds me of how change demands.
I sit here, still and thankfully,
blessed for all eternity.

5. Sit quietly for a few minutes when finished, feeling the quiet confidence swell inside. Really feel the emotion, knowing you can recapture it anytime you need it.

FINDING THE PERFECT HOME

This phase of new beginnings is the perfect time to set an intention for finding that new home you've been dreaming of. Kick the dreams to the curb, and take action to make it happen. When the New Moon beckons, set aside some time to bask in her energy and say quietly or aloud:

New Moon, new day, new house I pray,
My search is not yet done.

New Moon, new day, new nest I pray,
Where heart and hearth are one.

New Moon, new day, reveal I pray
That castle I'll call home.

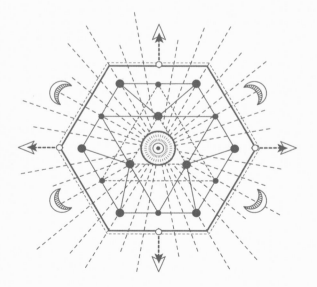

BLESS THIS HOUSE
OR APARTMENT

In this phase of new beginnings, there is no better time to bless and cleanse your new space. This two-phase process first clears negative energy and bad vibes, then fills the space left with positive, joyful intentions.

1. Gather the necessary materials and perform a smudging ritual (see page 117) to cleanse the space, paying special attention to corners, closets, and doorways. As you travel through the house, visualize the smoke carrying any negativity up and out with it. Extinguish your smudge stick fully before proceeding.
2. Gather some salt, bread, wine, and a few coins and assemble them on your altar, a table, or any space available. Take a moment to be still. Close your eyes and visualize yourself happy and productive in your new space. Breathe naturally. When you feel ready, say quietly or aloud:

   With this new home my need to roam has now come to an end.
   In this cleansed space, a brand-new life is one that I will tend.
   With salt for flavor, bread for health, wine for happy times,
   I cast these coins about my realm—life's riches will be mine.
   Please bless this house for in its midst life lived will be sublime.

3. Take a moment to thank the Moon for her energy and make a toast to your new home with the bread and wine.

HEALING

The Full Moon is optimal for healing, but the New Moon and Waxing Moon phases should not be overlooked.

Feeling the full weight of the Moon's energy, breathe deeply to fill your body from head to toe with her warmth. Reflect on what needs to be healed and create a picture in your mind of what that looks like. Keeping the picture in focus, when ready, say quietly or aloud:

> *Goddess Moon, tend to me in this time of ill.*
> *May your light mend my heart and help my mind be still.*
> *Bring me peace that I may use my energy to heal,*
> *Goddess Moon, shine on me that better I may feel.*

Or,

> *Silvery Moon, beacon of hope,*
> *Light my path to well.*
> *Moonbeams bright, sea of light,*
> *Cast a healing spell.*

When finished, remain quiet and remind yourself of the picture you had in your head. Take a moment to honor your courage and thank the Moon for her light.

WELCOMING A NEW PET

A new pet definitely means a new beginning . . . new habits, new fun, new discoveries, new love, just to name a few. Use the light and energy of the New Moon to recognize and welcome this new family member.

Gather your squirming bundle in your arms and stand somewhere, inside or out, where the Moon's light will reach you. With admiration for the journey you are about to engage in, say quietly or aloud:

Mother Moon, it's joy we feel and love to warm our hearts.
This furry [feathered, finned, etc.] beast loves us no end and trusts we'll never part.
With wisdom dear and guidance kind,
please bless this brand-new friend.

LONG LIFE

It goes so fast, we want it to last forever, but know that the best life is one lived in the moment each day . . . no matter how long. Use the latent energy of the New Moon to cast this spell, say quietly or aloud:

New Moon, walk with me on this journey.
May your ever-steady presence remind me of this promise:
To fill each day with love that fills my life with joy, so, come the day—
good-bye I say—I'll have lived life to its fullest.

HEALING GRIEF

As the Moon begins a new phase, consider, when you're ready, how her healing powers may help soothe an aching soul. When you're ready, say quietly or aloud:

This is the hardest thing I've done—my grief does overwhelm.
For loss has changed my life in ways before not ever known.

I sit, fair Moon, before your grace and wonder at your sight,
will beauty touch my life again—beyond this fleeting sight?

The Moon, she answers, "Yes, it will." And time, it helps to heal.
Return each night. We'll gaze—delight—at what God's plan reveals.

FINDING INSPIRATION

The Moon has inspired more things than you can even list. Do you think she might be willing to share a little of that? Say quietly or aloud:

To gaze upon your lovely face is said to bring desire,
from which, it's said, of heart and head you readily inspire.

Please turn your gaze upon my life to quicken its desire,
to find the words, or thoughts, or ways to create again untired.

PLANNING A VACATION

You can turn a Moon dance (see page 126) into a party, but sometimes a vacation can rejuvenate like nothing else. Say quietly or aloud:

New Moon, you travel through the sky, across its endless seas.
With map I stand, without a plan, but journey beckons me.

A spark ignite—to set aglow ideas that will inspire—
to pack a bag and venture forth with curious desire.

ABUNDANCE

An abundant life can mean different things—friends, love, money, learning . . . whatever abundance you want to invite in today, whisper this to the New Moon—and remember—everything comes to you as you need it, so be patient:

So starts your phase from New to Full, and brightly you do grow.
Imbue my world with bounty full and riches by the hour.

GROUNDING MEDITATION

As the New Moon begins her growth through a new phase, take the opportunity to ground yourself both in her balancing effects and in the Earth's energy to be truly present in your life.

If you have one, garnet is a great stone for its grounding energies. Hold it, while sitting or standing comfortably within view of the Moon, close your eyes, and open your mind to her stabilizing force. Feel your connection to the ground under your feet or in the chair where you sit. Let yourself relax and sink deep into that connection. When ready, say quietly or aloud:

I seek a place to set my roots to deepen as they grow.
To feel the ground beneath my feet and in the present know,
That with my strength and clarity, the heavens I may reach
To use my gifts for all their worth, dear Moon, I do beseech.

WAXING MOON
SPELLS

ILLUMINATE
INTENTIONS;
BUILD STRENGTH,
CONFIDENCE,
ENERGY, AND EXCITEMENT

HOPE IS ITS
OWN KIND OF MAGIC

The Waxing Gibbous Moon is full of potential energy in which we can visualize our intentions growing. To keep hope alive, and energy flowing, use this simple spell—say it quietly or aloud:

Waxing Moon, growing light,
Ignite the burn of hope's delight.
For hope does still, encourage a will
To blossom bold and bright.

FORGET ME NOT

The waxing phase is perfect for instilling the intention of growing memories—be they long lost, loved and lost, or any other type in between. Hold some rosemary, rose quartz, or lovely forget-me-nots if you can, to encourage a stronger charm, and say quietly or aloud:

The sweetness of your scent is near. I wake—it's just a dream.
For life, that time, was so sublime, whenever you were near.
I think of you most every day, and hope you do the same.
A wish, I pray, please, just this day, remember me again.

WISHES COME TRUE

You can always wish upon a star, but inviting the Moon in can help wishes come true faster! Say quietly or aloud:

Whether Moon, or star, or rainbow be—the pot of gold is there for me.
I wish I may, I wish I might, find my wish come true before the night
Doth curl its head upon the bough and sing sweet lullaby—rest now.

SUCCESS

A little success can put you over the Moon. But if it's a boost you need, speak to her—I'm sure she'll listen. Say quietly or aloud:

Fortune, fame, accomplishment; victory, profit, thrive.
Happy, healthy, prosperous; win, prevail, arrive.
Advancing Moon, instill in me success as you define.

LIVING JOYFULLY

Say quietly or aloud:

O' growing Moon, enrich my world with light that I may see,
That beauty, truth, and simple joys abound from sea to sea.
The choices made of how I see mean life lived joyfully.

NEW ADVENTURE

Feeling the need to spread your wings or satisfy that need for adventure? Open your heart to the Moon's inspiration to set you on your way. Say quietly or aloud:

Gentle Moon, navigating the heavenly seas,
Your itinerary must, this wanderlust appease.
With plan in hand and mind set free,
Sail on that I might follow thee.

PEACEFULNESS

This is a tall order, and this simple spell can be useful for you—to raise positive vibrations around you—but also to send out into the world, if you desire. Use the Waxing Moon to set your intentions for peaceful living, then recite the following, quietly or aloud:

> *Waxing Moon, your growing light shines bright from up above.*
> *Raising hopes, instilling dreams of peaceful times to come.*
> *Direct your gaze, with healing love, on all who see you now,*
> *That light may spark a single heart to action as a dove.*

Take a moment to thank the Moon for her help and be grateful for peace as it is.

EASING ACHES AND PAINS

When minor pains distract from your everyday joy or just get in the way of productivity, seek the Moon's healing warmth to ease them. Imagine the Moon's beams gently falling on the area in pain. Feel the warmth radiate through. When ready, say quietly or aloud:

> *When aches do slow and pain does grow, I conjure up the sight,*
> *Of warm Moon's glow, and faeries, lo, fair leaping with delight.*
> *O' soothing rays and joyous sight, bring healing with your light.*

FERTILE BLESSINGS

If it's the pitter-patter of little feet beckoning you, the Goddess Moon is surely on your side. For this spell, you may also wish to enlist the help of some of the goddesses worshipped for their fertility prowess . . . Isis, Freya, Arianrhod, and Diana, to name a few.

Gather any tools you want to work with, such as mustard or myrtle, or moonstone, perhaps a candle, and create an altar under the Waxing Moon. Take a moment to feel the Moon's growing light fill you with the energies you need to grow and tend a new life. Focus on your intentions. When ready, say quietly or aloud:

I stand here now, emotions high, with grateful outstretched arms—
May fruitful be my wish to thee, that pregnant do I grow.
My hopes and fears, I offer here, the rest I cannot know.
O' Goddess Moon—be boy or girl—please ply your magic charms.

INTUITION

The Waxing Moon's vibrational energy can heighten your natural intuition. Whether your intuition needs a boost from a slump, or you need reassurance to trust what it's telling you, try this spell.

Standing or sitting quietly, close your eyes. Let your mind be still and listen to what your heart is telling you. Unsure what that is? Say quietly or aloud:

> *Cleansing Moon, cast your light—dispense the shadows nigh.*
> *I call on you to heed my cry, awaken sights within.*
> *Power my internal eye, make clear what I deny.*

HOW CHARMING!

When you just can't find the right words to convey how you feel, this simple spell can help you turn on the charm. Take a moment to visualize the target of your enchantment. Take a deep calming breath and, when ready, say quietly or aloud:

> *Beguiling Moon, bewitching Moon, my heart has found the one.*
> *With words of charm, and airs mystique,*
> *May mesmerizing words I seek,*
> *Flow freely off my tongue.*

SOME PEOPLE
HAVE ALL THE LUCK

Try this simple spell during one of the Moon's waxing phases, when energy and excitement are building and have the power to spur you on.

Gather a gold or an orange candle and some matches. Sit comfortably in sight of the Moon. Place the candle on a heatproof surface and light it. Take a moment to let its light fill you with optimism as you release any negative thoughts. Say quietly or aloud:

> *This flame I see burns bright and free,*
> *May luck's abundance return to me.*

Extinguish the candle and take a moment to acknowledge all in your life you are lucky for.

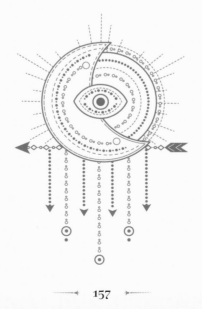

FRIENDSHIP

If it's companionship you yearn for, the Waxing Moon can be your spell's best friend.

Gather a red or pink candle and matches. Sit comfortably in a quiet place and light the candle on a heatproof surface. Gaze at the flame. Let your mind be free while the light fills you with peace. Taking long slow breaths—in and out—visualize activities you would do with your new friend, someone like-minded who enjoys what you do. When you feel ready, say quietly or aloud:

O' goddess of love and Goddess Moon, cast your hearts wide open.
May love spring forth to fill my life with friendship deep and true.
I pledge to give as much as receive, with friendships blessed and new.

Repeat as many times as you like. Let the candle burn down as you continue to visualize you and your new friend together. Keep your energies open to meeting new people.

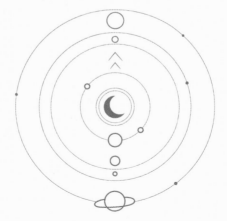

GET CREATIVE!

The waxing phase of the Moon is your time for creative action. You've set your intentions and started the process, so don't let anything get in your way of fulfilling your desires. Now is the time to pump up your energy and let your creative spirit fly. Opal, ylang-ylang, and the color yellow are all potential boosters for the ideas and imagination you seek.

1. Remind yourself of the intentions you've set.
2. Working with any crystals, herbs, oils, or other tools you'd like, place them on your altar. Sit quietly and focus your attention on their beauty (scent, color, shape, whatever you see) and let your thoughts flow freely.
3. Which thoughts inspire action? Which inspire new ideas? Which inspire more thought? Write these down in your journal for further meditation work.
4. When you are ready, say quietly or aloud:

Moon's bright light holds rainbow hues,
an endless well of changing views.
The shapes and shadows cast about
are ever-changing signs, no doubt,
That life does shift and life does show,
For new ideas to bloom and grow,
must first begin with faith and you—
To sow, to feed, to act, to reap,
no time to waste—just take the leap.
The Moon will light the way.

COURAGE TO TAKE ACTION

The Moon's waxing phase is the time to take action—and sometimes that requires a bit more courage than we have. You've been planting, nurturing, and growing the seeds of your intentions. With their imminent bloom, you may be wondering whether you've been putting your energies toward the right task. Trust your instincts and the illuminating Moon to help you see things through to their natural outcome. For a bit of extra courage, cast this simple spell. Fennel, thyme, basil, and aquamarine are all tools you can work with, if you like.

Under the light of the Waxing Moon, stand peacefully and gratefully for the chance to receive her gifts. Focus on the intention you've set or the questions you have. When ready, say quietly or aloud:

> With open heart and ready spirit, I seek your wisdom.
> With open mind and ready hand, guide my actions.
> With open eyes and ready courage,
> I'll take the path less known.
> Goddess Moon, your beacon lights my path
> to blessings yet unknown.

Take a moment to breathe in the light and fill your inner well with courage and confidence.

FULL MOON
SPELLS

ENERGY, CELEBRATE,
GIVE THANKS,
ABUNDANCE

HEALING ENERGY

The Full Moon is a powerful time for healing, and this spell will help cleanse your body of what hurts or ails. New Moon and Waxing Moon phases are also good times to repeat this.

Create a spell jar: Gather a small lidded jar, a personal item—one that represents your illness or pain—a piece of paper and a pen, and some liquid (Moon Water, see page 125, or wine, for example).

On the paper, write your intention, be it healing physical or emotional pain or finding peace and acceptance to some problem. Be specific. Fold the paper three times over and place it, your personal item, and the liquid into the jar. Seal the lid.

Holding the jar, stand, if you are able, or sit under the Full Moon's bathing light. Let it cover you like a warm blanket. Breathe in slowly, feeling the warmth travel through your lungs and down your torso, into your toes. Exhale slowly, feeling your breath carry away the pain up and out through your scalp. Repeat until you feel calm and centered, focusing on your breath—in, out. When ready, say quietly or aloud:

Healing Moon, I beseech thee, at this time of ill.
Send your light, let peace instill.
I pray your blessings from above,
Will fill my life with healing love.

Repeat the ritual as needed. Bury the jar when you feel better and are able to let the pain go.

AN ENERGY BOOST FOR YOUR FAVORITE SPORTS TEAM

Gather a clear quartz (recently charged by a Full Moon, if possible; see page 72) for maximum energy and ability to transmit your vibrations into space, and an object representing your team (jersey, hat, photo, etc.). Place the crystal on the object and take a minute to connect your energies with the crystal. When ready, say quietly or aloud:

Brilliant crystal, heed my plea,
Let the game be won by three.
More than three, a blessing be,
Brilliant crystal, heed my plea.

Repeat three times. Take a moment to visualize a celebration and thank the crystal for its work.

ROMANTIC LOVE

You cannot control another's will with your love spell, but you can send them a love note via the Universe's energies, or open the pathways to your heart to receive love. It will be felt as a subconscious hug, strengthening the connection you have. The Full Moon is a perfect time to invite the energy of abundant love into your heart and connect to that special someone.

Gather a piece of red construction paper, scissors, a black or gold indelible pen, rose quartz or ruby, matches and a flameproof bowl, and a red rose. A picture of your intended is optional.

1. Place the items on a heatproof surface, making an altar.
2. Cut out a heart shape from the red paper—any size you like.
3. Write the name of your beloved in the center of the heart and draw three lines underneath it.
4. Fold the heart in half along the center line and write your name on each half, on the outside of the heart, surrounding your intended with loving energy.
5. Holding the paper heart and chosen crystal to your heart, take a moment to visualize your love. When ready, say quietly or aloud:

Passionate crystal, be charged with my love. Join hearts and minds, alike.

6. Place the paper heart in the bowl and light it with the matches. Imagine the flames igniting love and desire in your intended, carrying your message through the cosmos.
7. Extinguish the flame and take a minute to hold the crystal and feel its loving vibration.
8. Place the rose in a vase by your bed and the crystal under your pillow. Repeat the spell and dream of your love.

DRAWING SOMEONE
SPECIAL TO YOU

If you want to gain the attentions of someone who's caught your eye to see if sparks may fly, use this bewitching spell.

1. Gather two rosebuds (just the blooms) of the same color and carefully remove the petals from each.
2. Line a large plate with paper towels and mix the petals together so you don't know which bud is which. Cover the petals with another paper towel and microwave on high power for 2 minutes. Keep an eye on them. Turn the petals over and re-cover. Microwave for 1 minute longer. If they are not completely dried, microwave in 15- to 30-second intervals, checking after each one, until dried.
3. Put the dried petals in a glass dish or sachet bag and add a small rose quartz or garnet, then a drop or two of rose essential oil, if you wish.
4. Place the dish under the Full Moon's light. Take a moment to picture your chosen. When ready, say quietly or aloud:

Full Moon, infuse these petals with your energy and light.
Full Moon, bewitch this crystal that its message does take flight.
Full Moon, enchant my spirit that enticement it ignites.

Take a moment to thank the Moon and imagine your sparks flying out into the Universe. Keep the petals out where you can see them and repeat the spell as desired.

GOOD LUCK

Dill—and the color green—are thought to bring luck. Using
the energy of a Full Moon offers the help of gravity's pull at its
strongest to absorb the power of good luck. Invoke this simple
spell when you feel the need for a boost in the luck category.

Gather some dill seeds, a large clay pot, some potting soil,
gravel, and water. Take everything outside and stand in the
Moon's light (a Full Moon has the most energy potential). Focus
your thoughts on the area in which you'd like a lucky strike to
occur. Be specific and imagine it happening.

Add a bit of gravel to the pot for drainage. Fill the pot with
soil and sprinkle the seeds over the soil. Cover with a light
dusting of soil to keep them in place. As you water the seeds,
say quietly or aloud:

Magnificent Moon, I ask your energy to warm these seeds
that my luck may grow as abundantly and fearlessly as they.
Thank you for your nurturing light.

Place the pot in a warm area where it will receive sunlight—in
addition to Moonlight—where the seeds should sprout in about
ten days. Check on the seeds periodically and water when dry.
Feel your luck grow as the dill stems grow ever higher.

Use the fresh herbs for any number of dishes, from soups to
pickles, to potato salad and salmon, and sprinkle some luck into
your everyday meals.

CLARITY

The Full Moon is a time for seeing fully and clearly. If you're feeling a bit muddle-headed and just need some help shaking out the cobwebs, try this spell:

In Full Moon I stand, seeking a hand,
to wipe the fog from my eyes.
So clearly I see what matters to me
and actions to meet, thus required.
Full Moon, take my hand—help me understand,
to realize my dreams and desires.

GIVING THANKS

The Full Moon fills us to the brim. Take a moment to give thanks and a nod of gratitude for the bounty in your life—then pass it on. Say quietly or aloud:

I thank you, Moon, for all you do to guide and comfort me.
I thank you, friends, for all you give—your love, support, and glee.
And so I stand beneath your light with heart so full of love,
To know my life is blessed, you see, without you I have none.

HELPING OTHERS

As we've learned, spells are unable to influence others, but, rather, are self-directed. That doesn't mean you can't cast a spell to help you recognize and step up when meeting others in need. To widen your view, bringing others into focus, call on the Full Moon's brilliance to help. Say quietly or aloud:

Gentle orb of abundance,
Whose force does balance Earth,
Reveal to me that I may see,
My gifts to heal the dearth.

FAIR WEATHER

Whether for a wedding, travel, sports event, or day off, beautiful weather is always welcome. Check in with the Full Moon for some help with the forecast. Say quietly or aloud:

Fair Moon—fair breeze, fair weather make,
That all upon this day may take
Delight in this day made to celebrate!

FEELING POWERFUL

Can you feel the power? No? Well, turn to the powerful Full
Moon for a boost of energy to have what it takes. Say quietly
or aloud:

There's power in numbers, but this time just one.
Full Moon, help me gather the courage that I need,
To show them the power is, yes, mine indeed!

MARRIAGE PROPOSAL

A Full Moon can bring out the full depth of love in us. If a
proposal is on your mind and you'd like to hurry it along, try
pleading your case to the Moon. (You can also try this if you're
gathering the nerve to make that proposal!) Say quietly or aloud:

Sparkling Moondust glitters and glows,
while magical Moonlight tickles my toes.
Happy and loved I feel when with you.
If married we be, I know we will grow
From one into two, and more may there be,
to bask in our love as a new family.

BEING OPEN-MINDED

When you start to disagree with someone, ask a question instead. Open your mind and heart to go with the flow, learn new things, and see things from another's perspective.

Fill a small bowl with cool water and add a couple drops of your favorite essential oil to lift your spirits. Close your eyes, dip your fingers in the water, and swirl them around. Feel the calming softness of the water and inhale the lovely fragrance. When ready, say quietly or aloud:

> *Bright-lit Moon, enlighten me to listen more than talk,*
> *For doing so can caring show, remove a stumbling block.*
> *For fear can make us disagree when really we do share,*
> *A love of peace, humanity, and harmony so rare.*

SALT SPELL
FOR HOME PROTECTION

Salt, especially Himalayan salt (see page 71), is imbued with the Earth's energies. Combine that with the Moon's for a powerful spell to protect your home.

Fill a small dish with salt and place it under the Full Moon's light, overnight, to blend their energies. The next day, walking clockwise (see page 48) around your home's perimeter or the perimeter of a room, carry the salt and say, quietly or aloud:

Moon and Earth, join energy to keep this home in sight,
That safe we be, no harm to see, by daylight or by night.

You can, if you like, sprinkle a bit of salt around the perimeter of your home outside, but beware too much may be harmful to lawn and plants.

FINDING SOMETHING LOST

Think of the Full Moon as a supercharged flashlight whose gravitational pull can help pull you toward that item you've misplaced . . . including your way! Try it!

Tides of Nature heed your cry, and swiftly they obey.
Cast your beaming rays this way to help me with this plea,
For lost again, this thing I need is set not in its place,
Return to me, Moon's gravity, what's lost in time and space.

WANING MOON
SPELLS

REFLECTION, LEARNING,
RELEASING ANYTHING
NOT HELPFUL,
REST, RENEWAL

BANISHING BAD

During the Moon's Last (Third) Quarter phase, use this spell
to cast away anything keeping you from realizing your goals and
banish negativity from your existence. Perform a simple sage
smudge (see page 117) or use some sage spray (see page 119) to
dispel bad vibes, as you wish.

In a quiet place in view of the Moon, take a moment to set
your intentions. When ready, say quietly or aloud:

> *Your light grows dim, but do not fear.*
> *It guides us still, when dreams appear.*
> *Tho' some say nay, or block the way,*
> *Be banished here and stay away.*

REPELLING THE ENEMY

What better time to rid your world of anyone with intent to do
harm. Once identified, don't wait. Restore order and balance
to your world with the Moon's cleansing energies. With a clear
threat in mind, and intentions focused, say quietly or aloud:

> *Goddess Moon, warrior of night, I plead my case to thee.*
> *With threat of harm, extend your arms, safely encircled I be.*
> *Protect and soothe, give strength to fight what does not strengthen me.*

Pause a moment to acknowledge the Moon for her strength and
feel the determination in you grow.

PATIENCE AND UNDERSTANDING

Not everyone thinks or acts as we do. But we learn so much
from the differences in our world when we just take the time.
For those days when you feel a bit off-kilter compared to
everyone else, seek balance in the Moon's soothing glow.
Say quietly or aloud:

In quiet light, I stand in peace; I listen for the words.
With quiet mind, I hear the hymn of life unfold its tune.
Of quiet heart I am, and know, you'll help me find the rhythm,
For sing us all, with different words, a song in unison.

RELATIONSHIP TROUBLES

This may be something you've been reflecting on and living your most positive life to resolve. During the waning phase, align with the fading energies to slow down and search deep within, to ask yourself what it is you want versus what you have. How can you take steps to make the two meet?

In this time of uncertainty, our self-talk can get negative. Use the Moon's gorgeous glimmer to see your beauty within and out. Try this affirmation when you need a little self-love:

> *Mother Moon, hold me tight; wipe away my tears.*
> *Let me look upon your face that I can clearly see—*
> *I am worthy. I am loved. I am ready. I am me.*
> *I am grateful. I am strong. I am someone. I am me.*

Take a moment to congratulate yourself for showing up today, as hard as it may be, knowing tomorrow will give you another chance.

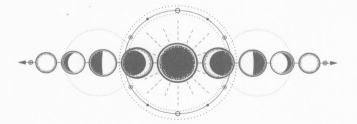

FORGIVENESS

Forgiveness can be hard to come by, especially when it comes to forgiving yourself. Try this simple spell when your heart is heavy and forgiveness is the only path to healing. It is your gift to you. The Last (Third) Quarter Moon is an especially good time to invite forgiveness into your life.

The heady scent of a rose can calm the nerves and heal feelings of anger and resentment, which can open your heart to healing and forgiveness. Likewise, rosemary, typically known as the plant of remembrance, can be used to keep good memories near, while releasing those that are hurtful. Invite forgiveness into the space they leave.

Gather a small bunch of fragrant roses (even one rose will do) or fresh rosemary. In the Waning Moon's light, hold the flowers or herb close to your nose. Breathe in deeply and slowly, visualizing the healing fragrance filling you up and absorbing any negative thoughts or feelings you have. Exhale slowly, feeling your breath release the negativity. Continue to breathe in and out until you feel calm and centered. When ready, say quietly or aloud:

With all that is fresh and new,
I open my heart to forgive.
Guiding Moon, please light the path that brings me to acceptance.
I breathe these scents that cleanse my pain,
which, pray, now fill with joy.
I am loved. I am enough—and I forgive.

INSIGHT/PROBLEM SOLVING

The dark of the waning crescent phase is a time when things naturally slow. The Moon's energizing light is at its lowest volume. Now is the perfect time to take stock of the results of your intentions this lunar cycle and seek wisdom in solving problems still with you. Recite this spell when you need to see through the darkness and into the light of truth.

Restful Moon, whose darkness falls upon this day,
Give time to shine this light of mine on thoughts I've kept at bay.
May wisdom bloom, and truth be known
That problems fall away.

FAMILY BLESSINGS

In this natural period of rest and renewal, now is the time to reconnect with friends and family you may have neglected during busier times. This simple spell can help you send loving vibrations out into the Universe. Say it quietly or aloud as many times as you like, and keep watch for what returns to you.

In times of darkness, friendships shine bright.
In times of darkness, family holds tight.
In times like these, when Moon's light wanes,
tend carefully to love that sustains.
O' Goddess Moon, O' mother of night,
shine tenderly your protecting light.

REVISING YOUR RESUME

Maybe you've set your intentions at the New Moon to find a new job and are busy with all that requires. The Waning Moon's period of reflection is a great time to dust off the resume so it shines as brightly as you do!

Journaling about your likes, dislikes, achievements, challenges, goals, and objectives as well as specific areas you'd like to grow and improve can be a great brainstormer for polishing your resume.

This can be a tough task, so, before you begin, send this affirmation toward the Moon, that she returns her light and sparkle to you:

I am courageous.
I am creative.
I am hardworking.
I am unique.
My talents will contribute—in every way they can.
My resume is just the start of showing who I am.

Take a moment to be grateful for your uniqueness and get to work revising that resume.

SPELL TO DE-STRESS

In addition to performing a soothing ritual, such as Moon bathing (see page 126), or working with your calming crystals (see page 62), this basic spell can help ease your nerves and quiet your soul when there's not time for more. While aligning with the Waning Moon can help your release, use this any time you need to refocus and stay calm.

Take a moment to sit quietly and be still. Close your eyes to shut out any distractions. Focus simply on your natural breathing, being present in the peaceful moment you've created. When ready, say quietly or aloud:

> *As darkness harkens, fears increase.*
> *I know not why or how.*
> *I seek your calm; I pray your peace,*
> *protecting Moon above.*
> *May gentle light help ease my fright*
> *and soothe my troubled soul.*

Meditate peacefully for as long as you need, feeling the calm grow within—cement the feeling so you can pull it up any time it's needed. When you're ready, gently return your senses to your surroundings and sit quietly, then make with a cup of Moon Tea (see page 130), until you are ready to rejoin the day.

SEEKING WISDOM

There are those times when just the facts are not enough. You must also have the wisdom and knowledge of what to do . . . or not do . . . with the information. Understanding the hidden implications of information and messages, and acting on them appropriately, sometimes means calling on a higher power.

When those moments face you, offer the following (quietly or aloud) to the wise Moon, and be open to her illuminating messages:

O' knowing Moon, I seek your help, for sagely must I see,
My head says, "Yes," my heart says, "No"—my friends, not one agrees.
With choices hard, and outcomes real, please wisely advise me.

ATTITUDE ADJUSTMENT

We all experience them—those times when negativity begins to drag us into the mire. When a quick change of attitude is really all that's required to reverse the course of your mood, try this cheerful spell:

Moon's beaming face
Breathes joyous words at night.
Listen for the glistening Moondrops.

AGING GRACEFULLY

Growing older is one of life's great joys. Don't be tempted to fight Nature's plan. When it gets you down or you start to give in to the fears, embrace the Moon's knowing grace. Say quietly or aloud:

You look the same today, as the day that you were born.
How do you do it, Goddess Moon? Please tell your secrets now.
My list grows long of aches, of pains, of wrinkles and repairs; of graying hair—
I sit and stare and wonder where I've gone.
Though I may look a wee bit different in face than that before,
I'm here, inside, with childlike eyes that see wonder in your every turn.

SWEET DREAMS

When night pulls her gentle curtain across the sky, summon the Waning Moon to tell her stories of peaceful dreams. Say quietly or aloud:

Your night's warm glow, its lovely show, does softly ease my fears.
As sleep draws nigh, I hear your tales, soft-whispered in my ears.
That dreams they bring do carry me, so gently, to that land,
Of nod and doze, in calm repose, I slumber like a bear.

CLEARING
A CLUTTERED MIND

When you just can't shake those worries loose, it's time for a bit of mental housekeeping. The Waning Moon is the time to pack up those mental troubles and let them go. Amethyst, with its soothing energies, can help. Holding the stone, take a few deep, calming breaths. Focus on the worries you'd like to release and let the stone absorb them. When ready, say quietly or aloud:

Worries, woes, and burdens, I release you into this stone.
I fill my cleared mind with the Moon's restorative powers.

Place the stone near a window where the Moon's cleansing energies will clear the stone and recharge it for your next use. Do this as often as needed to keep anxiety away.

WEIGHT LOSS

Dropping some unwanted weight might require dropping a few bad habits, too, or at least releasing whatever is holding you back from achieving your goals. Spend some time reflecting on what's standing in your way. When ready, say quietly or aloud:

Knowing Moon, in quiet times, I seek your tender voice,
I'd like to lose some weight, my friend, which does require choice.
Please help me fill my mental plate with filling words of praise,
And choose those healthy habits that will whittle down my waist!

SELECTING
A CHILD'S NAME

Seek the Moon's guidance for just the right moniker for your little bundle of joy—that this child may live happily ever after.

Of prince, or lord, or princess be;
this royal name I seek for thee.
O' Moon of thoughtful waning light,
lend sweet help to solve this plight.
For son or daughter yet to be,
to crown you with a name that's right
To live life rich and purposefully.

GROWING AN
ABUNDANT GARDEN

While planting under the Moon's light can be a little impractical, seeking her blessing for a bountiful harvest is a wise and practical thing.

In fertile ground I plant the seeds for bounty at my table.
To water, weed, and nurture full with sunlight's warming food.
In Moonlight may they sleep and dream to grow each day to be
A harvest I can share and feed to answer hunger's need.

Though gently folding pages closed
May signal it's the end,
But wait; don't go, the Moon, oh-ho,
Now calls you a dear friend.
You've summoned strength and courage and love
To walk this magic path.
Now, hand in hand, rejoice—be glad,
The journey's just begun.

As above, so below.

ACKNOWLEDGMENTS

First, to Rage Kindelsperger, for asking me to take a leap of faith. And to Keyla Pizarro-Hernández and the rest of the Quarto (Wellfleet) team, for bringing it to life.

Grateful "thank yous" to Gaye Cassells and Julie Kerr, for their love, sisterhood, friendship, and encouragement and the magic those things can bring to one's life.

To Sharon D'Angelo, High Priestess and Intuitive Guide, for her enlightening discussion of Wicca and her generous and kind willingness to help. You can find her at www.sharondangelo.com.

And finally, to my husband, John, for the magic he brings to our world daily. When you cast your eyes in my direction, it was like . . . magic.

RESOURCES AND REFERENCES

To explore more of what the Moon and her magic have to offer, check out these informative resources.

American College of Healthcare Sciences: achs.edu

Aromatherapy.com

Aroma Web: aromaweb.com

Astrology Online: astrology-online.com

Baring-Gould, Sabine. Curious Myths of the Middle Ages, new ed. *London, U.K.: Rivingtons, 1876.*

Cajochen, C., S. Altanay-Ekici, M. Münch, S. Frey, V. Knoblauch, and A. Wirz-Justice. "Evidence that the Lunar Cycle Influences Human Sleep." Current Biology *23 no. 15 (August 5, 2013): 1485–8. doi:10.1016/j.cub.2013.06.029.*

Conscious Lifestyle Magazine: *consciouslifestylemag.com*

Color Meanings: color-meanings.com

Crystal Dictionary: crystaldictionary.com

Davis, Patricia. Astrological Aromatherapy. *London, U.K.: Random House U.K., 2004.*

EatingWell: eatingwell.com

eHow: ehow.com

Encyclopaedia Britannica: *britannica.com*

Energy Muse: energymuse.com

Kitchn: thekitchn.com

Law, S. P. "The Regulation of Menstrual Cycle and Its Relationship to the Moon." Acta Obstetricia Gynecologica Scandinavica *65, no. 1 (1986): 45–8.*

Mayo Clinic: mayoclinic.org

Museum of the Moon: my-moon.org/research

National Aeronautics and Space Administration: nasa.gov

National Geographic: *nationalgeographic.com*

Perrakis, Ph.D., Athena. Crystal Legends, Lore, and Myths, *Beverly, MA: Quarto, 2019.*

Psychology Today: *psychologytoday.com*

Sage Goddess: sagegoddess.com

Saveur: *saveur.com*

Sharon D'Angelo, High Priestess and Intuitive Guide: sharondangelo.com

Smithsonian: *smithsonianmag.com*

Space.com

Tarot.com

The Buddhist Centre: thebuddhistcentre.com

The Old Farmer's Almanac: *almanac.com*

The Weather Channel: weather.com

U.S. Games Systems, Inc. "Rider-Waite Tarot Deck" booklet. Stamford, CT. usgamesinc.com

Zodiac Arts: zodiacarts.com

INDEX